PRAISE FOR *What Cannot Be Undone:*
True Stories of a Life in Medicine

"By showing us what is often hidden behind a white curtain, Dr. Walter Robinson explains how to reconcile ourselves, as others have, to sickness and to health. Everyone who has ever sweated it out in a hospital waiting room should read this astonishing book."—Susan Cheever, author of *Home Before Dark*

"What are the limits of the power of doctors, and of human beings? When should we intervene, and when it is our job to watch and to accept? Reading Walter Robinson is like getting stories from a brilliant war correspondent. He's our man on the ground, and the ground is medicine, life, and death. A gorgeous and important book."—Joan Wickersham, author of *The Suicide Index: Putting My Father's Death in Order* and *The News from Spain: Seven Variations on a Love Story*

"Among physician authors, Dr. Robinson stands out for his ability to peel away the common clichés and tropes that populate so much of this literary genre, giving us unflinching insights into both the utterly mundane as well as the truly extraordinary experiences of physicians and patients alike."—Robert D. Truog, MD, director of the Center for Bioethics at Harvard Medical School and coauthor of *Talking with Patients and Families about Medical Error: A Guide for Education and Practice*

What Cannot Be Undone

RIVER TEETH LITERARY NONFICTION PRIZE

Daniel Lehman and Joe Mackall, Series Editors

The River Teeth Literary Nonfiction Prize is awarded
to the best work of literary nonfiction submitted
to the annual contest sponsored by *River Teeth:
A Journal of Nonfiction Narrative.*

Also available in the River Teeth Literary
Nonfiction Prize series:

The Rock Cycle by Kevin Honold

Try to Get Lost by Joan Frank

I Am a Stranger Here Myself by Debra Gwartney

MINE: Essays by Sarah Viren

Rough Crossing: An Alaskan Fisherwoman's Memoir
    by Rosemary McGuire

The Girls in My Town: Essays by Angela Morales

What Cannot Be

Walter M. Robinson

Undone

True Stories
of a Life
in
Medicine

University of New Mexico Press / Albuquerque

ISBN 978-0-8263-6371-8 (paper)
ISBN 978-0-8263-6372-5 (electronic)

Library of Congress Control Number: 2021948229

Founded in 1889, the University of New Mexico sits on the
traditional homelands of the Pueblo of Sandia. The original
peoples of New Mexico—Pueblo, Navajo, and Apache—
since time immemorial have deep connections to the land
and have made significant contributions to the broader
community statewide. We honor the land itself and those
who remain stewards of this land throughout the generations
and also acknowledge our committed relationship to
Indigenous peoples. We gratefully recognize our history.

Cover illustration: Marco Rosario Venturini Autieri /
    istockphoto.com
Designed by Mindy Basinger Hill
Composed in 10.5/15pt Minion Pro and
    Helvetica Neue LT Std 55 Roman

For Tom

CONTENTS

FOREWORD

Physicians have written about their patients since the advent of the profession, but the patients in these stories did not come to see me because they wanted to be in a story. They came to me for medical care, and that is what I provided to the best of my ability.

Because I want to respect their privacy, I have in these essays disguised patients' names and details in a manner that would make a journalist squirm: Sometimes I have combined two patients into one, sometimes I have given patients different families, sometimes I have rearranged the events of their care. I have put words in their mouths when I remember only the gist and nuance of what they said. I have changed the names and locations of my colleagues.

I have relied on my memory of events, and my memory is not perfect for all the details. Over the years, in trying to understand what it has meant to me to practice medicine, how it changed me as a person, I have told and retold these stories to myself in such a way that they have become the truth for me. And that is what I am seeking in this book—the truth about what it has meant to me personally to practice medicine over the course of many years. I stand by that effort, errors and all.

The truth about American health care would make a terrible television show. Illness and death on the screen are not like illness and death on the wards. People are often surprised when they become patients or when their family members have serious illnesses that things are not at all what they expected. It is easy to sacrifice hard truth for easy drama. I cannot compete with the tidy endings and the all-knowing fictional—and saintly—versions of physicians available on TV. As these stories show, I am no saint, no hero, no wizard. On my best days as a doctor, I was ordinary.

That the stories here depict more of the sorrow than the joy of a life with serious illness is attributable to the writer and his circumstances. There are plenty of happy stories about life with serious illness, many of them written by people who know it best. I urge the reader to seek those stories out. The patients and families in these stories had to contend with my imperfections as a doctor and a human while they taught me what it means to live gracefully in the face of hope and tragedy. For that, I thank them, one and all.

ACKNOWLEDGMENTS

Many people helped make these essays possible, but three people deserve special thanks: Susan Cheever, Ben Anastas, and Joan Wickersham. Susan Cheever had the wisdom to tell an overeducated physician to start over and keep going. Ben Anastas encouraged a weary man to get started writing again. Joan Wickersham taught a hesitant writer how to put just enough of himself on the page to make a good story. For being wonderful teachers and friends, I cannot thank each of you enough.

I would also like to thank my colleagues and fellow writers Denton Loving, Keith Lesmeister, Cassie Pruyn, Corina Zappia, Megan Galbraith, and Cathy Salibian for reading earlier drafts of these essays in spite of my repeated decisions to write mostly about things people would rather not discuss.

I would like the thank the editors of the journals that published my work, especially Christina Thompson at *Harvard Review*, who encouraged me more than she may know by calling one of my essays "harrowing (but in a good way)."

I would like to thank the Bennington Writing Seminars for changing my life for the better.

And thank you to Tom Bertrand, who makes everything worthwhile.

NOTE

Some of the essays in this book previously appeared, often in substantially different versions, in the following journals:

The Literary Review: "Nurse Clappy Gets His"

The Sun: "This Will Sting and Burn" (reprinted in *Reader's Digest*)

Harvard Review: "White Cloth Ribbons"

AGNI: "What Cannot Be Undone"

Ruminate: "White Coat, Black Habit"

What Cannot Be Undone

WHAT CANNOT BE UNDONE

A thick row of white tape secures the boy's arms to the steel armature above his head. Two nurses paint his scrawny chest with brown
disinfectant, starting at the center where the incision will begin and
arcing outward in practiced motions. The muscle relaxant flowing
at half a milligram per minute into his largest vein has uncoupled
his nerves from his muscles, but in spite of the drug's name he is not
relaxed, not sprawled out in confident slumber on a bed as other
fifteen-year-old boys might be. Children under anesthesia are not
asleep so much as absent, or so I had come to think because the idea
of masked strangers cutting open a sleeping body is a nightmare
not just for the sleeper. So my mind removes this child from the
scene, teleports him outside the normal, forward flow of time. Over
decades of being a doctor, I have come to embrace useful illusions.
Today, the illusion of this boy's absence during the surgery permits
me to acquiesce to the surgeon cutting his chest open.

Today the boy on the table is named Henry, and at the moment, a
tube erupts from his mouth and travels into the aperture of a vertical
accordion that rises and falls with a sigh as it delivers piston-precise
breaths of measured gas to his damaged lungs. Though his lungs are
hard with scars and infection, destroyed by cystic fibrosis (CF), the
machine's bellows do not strain under the work, and so as I stand
surveying his body, I wonder if this may be the first moment in years
that he has breathed without struggle. My hope is that these next
few hours will hold the last breaths he takes with his own lungs.

The room is white and warm, clean and orderly. I am grateful to be here among these hopeful people as together we write a new future for this boy.

Two days ago someone else, a stranger to me and to Henry, was struck in the head by a blunt object, a tree or a dashboard or a bullet. When the blow landed, the stranger's semisolid brain slammed back and forth inside the solid walls of his skull. As the blood vessels that travel through the fibrous sheath covering the brain were torn, blood began to fill his skull and push his brain to one side. Liquids and solids competed for space.

Or it may have been that his brain itself was torn by the blunt force, and that bits of brain now threatened to leak out through a broken skull.

Or this stranger may have had a weakness in the wall of an artery, either a single bulge like the first bubble of a clown's balloon dog, or perhaps a larger cluster like a swollen blackberry. Whichever it was, one of those weakened walls popped under the pulsing pressure of the heart, and blood began to push the brain up against the wall of the skull.

However it started, Henry and I needed stupendous luck for the stranger's story to become Henry's story. The right sort of someone else had to be there when the blunt force was applied, and they had to do the right sort of something about it. Someone had to see the injury or hear the violence, hear the thump of the body against the carpeted floor, and not just go about their business but decide to call the right number to alert the right people, and then those right people had to find the body and get it to the right sort of hospital. Once at the hospital, it had to be clear that the brain was damaged in just the right sort of way: Too little damage and the stranger would have survived; too much damage and the stranger would have died before we could harvest the organs.

At the time, I wouldn't have called it luck out loud, but everybody knows that's just what it is.

The surgeons have begun to work. After slicing through the smooth dark lines of disinfectant-painted skin, they have separated the muscles and fibrous tissue, pulled apart the edges of the body's covering down to the level of bone, and cauterized the bleeding in a harmony of movement and skill. The insistent beeping of the blue-tipped electric cautery quiets as the larger tools are placed in the surgeon's hands. The crisp crunch of the first bite by sterile shears on bone is a signal that the real operation has begun, and the final snip across the sternum releases Henry's rib cage from its constraint. The tension stored in the flexible strips of bone and muscle yanks his chest walls open to expose a heart embraced by wet lungs. The contents of his chest bloom into the clean air of the operating room.

Now the operating team can see directly what I have seen as shadows on X-rays and CT scans: his lungs are not the clean pink-beige of a healthy child, but are red and dark mounds crossed with uneven scars. Congealed blood and glue-like pus has oozed to the lungs' surface and stuck them to the inside of the chest wall. Over an hour of careful dissection will be necessary to free the old lungs from their cage. It will take an hour more before his chest is ready to hold the stranger's lungs that are still attached to that other body in a hospital a few hours away.

Some details of a donor's death are important. Limbs can be torn off or crushed if someone applies pressure and places a tourniquet. Broken bones or deep lacerations do not eliminate the stranger as a candidate for organ harvesting. A bit of diabetes and obesity, some alcohol use (not too much), arthritis or asthma, anxiety or alopecia or a history of appendicitis, all these we can manage. But cancer or serious infection would leave a mark on the lungs, and that won't do for our Henry.

Organ transplantation has an uneven rhythm, with measures of intense concentration interposed with prolonged pauses. When there is nothing to do but wait, I imagine the stranger's last day as

3

one of a dozen different movies. Maybe a motorcycle speeds along a curving country road on the last warm day of the fall, where wet leaves collect in the crook of a turn, and the acceleration of the machine and the body causes the wheels to lose their grip on the asphalt. Or perhaps a family car trip that begins in the warm sunshine is interrupted by a swerving truck no one sees coming. Perhaps a gun goes off unexpectedly, or not, after a dinner meant for reconciliation, or not. I am less interested in the plot than in the backstory. Was it fever and cough that made the motorcycle rider lose control? Had the driver of the family car seen the doctor that week for a rash? Was it a bad divorce that made the man pick up the gun, or was it a recent relapse back into heroin or news of a metastasis? I am alert to the sorrows that cling to the organs but indifferent to those that remain in the husk, the parts we will not use for Henry.

Those of us who care for Henry will call the stranger not by his name, but by his new role: "the donor." This is not because we do not know the donor's name—we do, and we may know more about him than his family does—but by convention we keep a wall between his tragedy and our boy. We want to give Henry a fresh start. We want the donor's slate to be washed clean of the residue of dying. On our best days, we see the donor as angelic in light of his gift. On our worst days, we curse the donor for having been a poor steward of his organs, for disqualifying himself by ruinous habits whose consequences he should have seen coming. We all know the unspoken truth: transplantation depends on the tragedies of strangers. I don't linger among the details of that tragedy.

Thirty minutes ago, I had been at the head of Henry's bed, using my right hand to drive a bronchoscope down through the tube in his mouth into his lungs while controlling the tip of the scope with my left hand. I pushed and pulled at a lever with my thumb to control the metal cables that run inside the scope, turning it left and right and craning my neck to see the video of the inside of the lungs on the screen mounted to the ceiling on the left side of the gurney. These semi-acrobatics were uncomfortable, but everything in the room must be positioned to give the surgeons room to work. I am not one of the surgeons, just one of the pediatricians, and so I made do.

My job was not hard, no biopsies or precision work. I had to use the scope to wash out the windpipe and its main left and right branches so the surgery to attach them to the new lungs would be slightly easier. I used a special cleaning solution, an enzyme that microscopically juliennes clumps of mucous sludge so it is thin enough to suck out through the scope. A dark and foamy slurry, verdant and rotten like the underside of a dying fern, filled a small round container called the mucous trap attached to the side of the bronchoscope. I had to change the trap three times as it became filled. I could have washed and suctioned for hours, but you cannot bail out the ocean with a teacup.

Earlier this morning Henry kissed his parents good-bye in the pre-op suite. They had come to the hospital after getting what we all call "The Call" from the transplant nurse. The Call has been the focus of this family's existence for the last eighteen months. We say to them, "When you get The Call . . ." and "When The Call comes . . ." We never say if.

The Call begins with the beeper going off. For families on the transplant list, the beeper is both a reminder that all the current therapies did not save their child and an electronic tether to a possible better future. They protect it, they worry its buttons with their fingers, they wonder if the batteries are still fresh. They jump when it goes off, they panic and scramble to answer it, fingers shaking as they dial the number on the luminous green screen. They forget it sometimes when they leave the house, and so they turn around and drive home as fast as they can to get it. The beeper commands loyalty.

Early this morning when the beeper went off, someone in the family spoke to the transplant coordinator while everyone else ran the list in their head of things they had been told: who they would see, what would happen first, how long it would take. This morning Henry was sick but not as sick as he could be—he had been out of the hospital for a month and was scheduled to go back in soon for his seventh course of IV antibiotics this year. The Call meant that this morning was the first morning since he was diagnosed as an infant that Henry hadn't started the day with thirty minutes of chest-physio treatments. His mother had to stop him from taking his pills—*nothing by mouth but water, remember?*—but he did a few nebulizer treatments while his parents were packing the car. It was a two-hour ride to the hospital, and he wanted to be able to sleep in the back seat with minimal coughing.

Did he think this was the last day that would begin with a head-ache and a cough? Did he think about the incision, the pain post-op, the drains and the tubes and the needles to come? Did he think of the future, of a life without coughing, a life like people without CF? Did he think about school or girls or boys or college? I don't know, because I didn't know Henry outside of the clinic, outside of his illness. I didn't know what he was interested in other than surviving. I should have tried to know him as a whole person, or so say the books on being a better doctor, but I don't think Henry really wanted this. What teenage boy, sick or not, wants to reveal himself to the paunchy middle-aged doctor? Bad enough that I asked him every time I saw him about his mucous and his stools. We had enough to talk about without getting hopes-and-dreams personal. This is what I did know: He followed my instructions. He obeyed me. He never fought against the treatments and schedules. He took his meds now, and he would take them after the transplant. He would keep his appointments. He was, as we say, "an excellent candidate for a transplant."

What, really, does The Call mean, when it comes? The family thinks it means Henry will get a new pair of lungs installed today, though we tell them over and over that this is not the way it works. The Call is only a signal to come to the hospital. The Call only means that someone who is about Henry's size and blood type in a nearby hospital has died in the right sort of way. The Call means only this: You should come here right now. We'll see what happens next.

Twenty-four hours ago, in a conference room off to the side of the intensive care unit of a hospital two states away from Henry, some other doctor had a meeting with the stranger's loved ones. She said what the loved ones surely knew: that the stranger could no longer breathe on his own without the machines. But it was worse than that, she would have said: his brain is so damaged that he is no longer alive.

His heart is beating and his lips are pink and his hands are warm to the touch, but he is dead, the doctor says. Not cold-blue-and-stiff dead but a special kind of dead, *brain dead*, a kind of being dead only possible since 1968 (though I hope she did not go into all this) when a group of doctors at Harvard decided that a brain that no longer worked in a rather specific way meant that you were dead enough to donate your organs even though you weren't dead enough to bury. Medicine needed this new kind of being dead because organs from cold-blue-and-stiff dead people are of no use to a transplant team.

And so the doctor wanted to ask permission to let a good thing come out of death, to harvest what was still useful from a tragedy. No doubt this was hard to hear, and harder to believe. I wasn't there to hear it, but I know from experience all the ways the conversation could have gone.

Some families will mention donating organs right away, before the doctor can even explain brain death; for them, the rescue of others relieves a portion of their sorrow.

Other families will say no, *he is still alive*, you doctors aren't trying to hard enough to save him. You doctors did this on purpose, they will say, because you want the organs for a patient you like better, someone richer or more important than our loved one.

Some families will ask for a priest or a pastor, who might say *yes* to donation because it is God's will to help others, or *no* because an intact body is needed in Heaven. Other priests or pastors will say *go ahead, organ donation is a special gift*. Some priests or pastors will say *it is all up to you*. Some priests or pastors will not know what to say; there is no page in their prayer book for this situation. Some families will order the priest out of the room after hearing the answer they don't want.

Some families will be silent in their shock and grief. Some families will be loud: their wailing will be heard though the conference room doors, and the ward clerk will hurry the families of other patients out into the hall or down to the cafeteria.

Some families will have to be shown the organ donor check mark on the driver's license. *It was his wish*, the doctors say. That will do for some families, but some families will say no when the card says yes. *He never wished for this, no matter what that card says*.

Some people have no families, so the doctors decide.

After the shock and the tears, or the sorrow and the relief—however they got there and believing whatever they believed about the right and the good—the family in that room said yes and signed the papers, and the process moved forward.

Once the decision is made to turn a patient into a donor, some families will leave the hospital, wanting to get away from the scene of the shock, riding down the elevators in silence and walking out of the lobby into the gray dawn. They will spend their day explaining what happened to everyone they meet.

Other family members will want to say good-bye. They will go back to the bed in the ICU and hold the warm hand of their beloved, waiting to witness a moment of dying, a final good-bye when the soul flies out over the bed and joins the waiting angels, a dividing line between alive and dead clearer to them than the doctor's words. They will ask each other whether his soul is still in the room. They will ask each other if he is already in Heaven. They will try, and fail, to think of him as already dead. They will stand one last time at his bed, surprised by how his life had come to this. They will stroke his cheek, lax and still except for the small shake of the ventilator. They will not know how to treat his body, looking alive and yet being dead. They will not know when it is time to say good-bye, because there is no moment, only the time they choose to leave, encouraged by the kind but firm nurse that it is time.

The newspaper will say he died the day the organs were removed, even though that might be the day after the declaration of brain death. The paper will read something like, "following a tragic incident, he was declared brain dead on Tuesday and died on Wednesday," acknowledging what ordinary people know, that being dead means funeral-and-gravesite dead, not dead-enough-to-donate-an-organ dead. The gravestone will list the date of the harvest. Brain death makes sense as an idea, but like democracy and love it's an idea that requires us to rearrange reality for its enactment; it is a good idea, as it helps people do the right thing in difficult times. But in the presence of the warm body and beating heart, brain death is slippery idea: we have to keep putting our good intentions in front of our sensations. Brain death insists that we see death with the eyes of the living. Everybody involved in transplantation knows the contradictions that cling to the idea of brain death, but we have agreed not to look at them too closely. We repeat the catchphrases that give us comfort: *Transplantation is the gift of life, Don't take your organs to Heaven*, and so on.

Henry and his family will struggle with their thoughts about the donor, who he was and what he and his family made possible. They both will and won't want the details of the donor's death, and we will guide them to think about the donor the way we do. The official policy is that both the donor and the recipient remain anonymous. Some donor families do not want to know who the recipients are, and some donor families want more than anything to know everything about the recipient. Some transplant organizations will facilitate anonymous letters back and forth between the donor and recipient families, but in the age of the internet, maintaining anonymity gets harder and harder. Today, Henry and his family have enough to think about.

Lungs cannot travel far. Lungs are delicate, three-dimensional bags of tiny balloons, each balloon held open by the pull of the balloon next to it, the whole interconnected mass designed to expand and contract inside the box of the rib cage. The lungs have their own immune system, their own defenses, their own chemistry.

Lungs cannot wait. Lungs can only last five hours outside a body. Even with all the advances in preservation and cooling of organs, there is a time limit. More than five hours, and the lungs begin to consume themselves; less than five, and the lungs will still work when the new blood of a new person flows through them. We count the five hours between the time that the surgeon at the donor's hospital clamps the arteries that supply blood to the lungs and the time that those clamps are released inside the new body. It takes time to sew the small veins and arteries onto the original heart's plumbing, time to get the flow right in the new vessels, time to make a sleeve of the new lungs' left and right main branches and sew them into the stumps of the original lungs. Time is why we have already gotten Henry ready in the operating room. We haven't got enough time to wait to start until the new lungs are in the room with Henry. Time is why the anesthesiologist has put all the central lines in Henry's neck already, why his chest has been scrubbed and washed and draped, why his arms have been taped up, why there is a tube in his bladder, in his mouth, up his nose. The surgeons must begin the surgery on Henry's old lungs now while the new lungs are being removed from the brain-dead/body-alive person two states away.

The surgeons are split into two teams. One team travels to remove the lungs from the brain-dead person; this is called the *harvest team* or the *procurement team*, but we usually just call them the *away team* as though this were *Star Trek*. The away team's job is not simply harvesting the lungs—they are looking at the chest X-rays, reading the chart, looking at the reports of anything sucked out of the lungs while they are still inside the donor. They are making sure the slate is clean enough to write Henry's new story. They are also jockeying for space and time with the donor's body, competing with the other away teams harvesting the other organs. Each team wants to remove their organ quickly to get it on the plane or in the ambulance. Each team has a different life they are trying to save somewhere else.

The *home team*, my team, is the *recipient team*. Our surgeon is alert at every moment to how the harvest is going in the other hospital, staging the surgery on the recipient step by step based on the reports of the harvest team. The old lungs must be freed from their bony cage, and then the scarring and infection of a lifetime must be carefully peeled away from the inside of the rib cage. Normal lungs glide inside the rib cage, floating on a thin layer of fluid with each breath, sliding past the inside layer of the ribs with each breath. But normal lungs do not need to be transplanted. In a person with cystic fibrosis sick enough to need new lungs, infection and scarring has invaded the clean and smooth space between the inside of the rib cage and the lung: the lung has adhered to parts of the chest wall, and new and tortuous blood vessels have grown into the space. Removing CF lungs is a detailed and bloody job, and it takes time.

The skill of the home team surgeon overwhelms me. He is a man I admire with the intensity reserved for a loved one. He is quiet and confident, serious and friendly, utterly dependable and yet never to be bothered with trivial things. Every day, I regret the times I bothered him or asked an obvious question. He is never arrogant like so many of his colleagues, though I have learned to forgive the others' their arrogance out of compassion for what it must do to them to have so much power. In one sense the transplant surgeon is like a god, reaching into the frail body to remove the dysfunction and disease, and pulling down a cure from the sky to remove all the suffering. Some of them succumb to the adoring worship of the civilians. How could they not? But they know that risk stalks their successes. The best ones train each other not to think too much of themselves. They hold each other to standards far higher than they hold me, a mere pediatrician. They are only as good as their last operation. And so they are on guard, the best ones, to see their role in the life and death of the patient, to see the contingency of their successes. They are trying to be good enough in a world that expects miracles on demand.

This surgeon has more than his allotted share of patience, some of which I regret he must spend on me. I am not confident enough in this work, not optimistic enough. I remember the deaths too clearly. I focus on the relapses, the infections, the complications, and the side effects. I could not lead a transplant team because my faith in the future is not strong enough. I like to think I can function as a serious and careful part of the team, but I am uncomfortable taking credit for any of the successes. I do not want to be thanked for saving a life, because I cannot block out my thoughts about how it might have been otherwise.

This is my flaw as a doctor. This surgeon has been kind enough not to mention it, though he sees it as surely as I do. In return, I do not mention what I suspect is his flaw: He hates to be present during a death. He hates to face the accusing eyes of a mother. He is too kind to force the hard truth on someone who will not hear it. It isn't that he doesn't have strength or courage—he has plenty of both. It's that he will not let himself get comfortable with tragedy. Being comfortable with tragedy is exactly what I *can* do. I can sit at the bedside and wait for the end. I can stand to be hated for the fact of mortality. I can keep saying the hardest truth.

So we make a good team, I think, though we have never discussed it. We do not want to share our insecurities; my fear might be contagious, and hope is the engine of a transplant team.

On this morning in this operating room, I am where I like to be: ready to help, but off to the side. The surgeon is doing his job, and I am sitting on a short stool on the left, my eyes at the level of the gurney so that all I can see are the backs of the surgical team. I watch the monitors and listen to the murmurs of the surgeons and the nurses. I go through my to-do checklist over and over. I answer calls from the inpatient wards about other patients, though I use a phone in the hall to do this. I do not want to tie up the operating-room (OR) phone line.

Things are going well: The harvest is in process at the other hospital, and Henry's lungs are being carefully separated from their inflamed box. The bleeding is controllable. Henry's heart is strong enough to suggest he will do well on the bypass machine when the time comes. There is only the steady sound of the anesthesia pump, the short humming of the cautery machine as the bleeding vessels are being singed and clotted, and the sounds of surgical instruments being handed back and forth. Everything is going according to plan.

Now there is a call to the room. The nurse answers it and says the away team needs to speak to the surgeon.

The surgeon gives a few moments of instruction with the surgical fellow and steps back from the operating field. The nurse puts the phone next to his still-masked face. I cannot see his expression, as his eyes are obscured by the special magnifying glasses all the surgeons wear during surgery these days, a pair of jeweler's loupes mounted to glasses, and his nose, mouth, and chin are behind the oval blue mask he prefers over the rectangular ones I wear. His gloved hands are clasped together in front of him to keep from touching any unsterile surface. He is still attached to the cord of the head lamp that rests on his surgical cap, and he knows not to look anyone in the eyes for fear of blinding them for a moment. I cannot read what he is hearing on his face. I do not know what is happening. No one seems worried.

He steps farther away from the stretcher and pushes his face closer to the phone. He twists his shoulders and cocks his head, his gloved hands now caressing the fingers of the other hands, and though he is wearing two pairs of gloves I can see him squeeze the blood out of the fingers of one hand with the other.

He says to everyone working on Henry, "I have to step out," and he pinches a fold out of the front of his surgical gown and pulls; the paper straps that secure the gown in the front and back rip with the pressure, and he pulls off his gloves inside the gown and wads the whole outfit up to toss in a wastebasket at the edge of the room. He unhooks from the power supply for the head lamp and pulls it off his head. He lets his loupe glasses fall to his chest on their neck strap. He takes the phone in his hand and walks to the edge of the room, listening and asking questions.

In a few minutes I will know exactly what he was hearing on the phone: At the other hospital, the surgeons have opened the chest of the donor and worked their way around the inside of the chest wall. To their surprise, there are pools of new and old blood. Crush injuries cover the outside surface of both lungs. Pieces of the lung are falling away in the harvesting surgeon's hands.

There must have been some unseen trauma to the chest when the donor died, maybe during CPR, maybe during the accident, maybe when he was intubated in the ambulance, maybe this, maybe that, no one knows. But there is damage to the lungs. Not enough damage to see on the scans, but too much damage to the lungs to survive what must come next: the removal, the dunking in cold solution, the flight to the next hospital, the handling needed to make the new connections to the old vessels and airways.

Too much damage for the lungs to be transplanted.

Certain death for the recipient if attempted.

Certain death for Henry.

But at the time all I see is the surgeon step back toward the stretcher, his face still covered by the round blue mask. His eyes are clear blue framed by wrinkles, and his blond hair is damp on his forehead through the surgical cap.

The room is suddenly quiet as everyone looks away from their tasks. The pressure in my ears changes, as though the molecules in the room had suddenly stopped moving and I were standing in a still lake where once there were waves. No one speaks. No one moves. We wait for the surgeon to explain.

"We have to stop now."

He explains the condition of the donor's lungs in short sentences. Everyone has questions that they do not ask. Everyone wants to talk him out of it, wants to figure out a solution, for the people in this room are used to a solution for every problem. But no one will object—there is no other decision, and we all know this by the time he gets to the end of the explanation. The decision is his to make. We cannot share that burden, only recognize it.

We will stop now.

The surgeon speaks with the fellows to explain how to begin closing the chest back up, how to pack the drainage tubes in like he planned, how to bring the ribs back in place like he planned, how to back out of the space they have begun to create for the new lungs and be gentle with the old ones. The living chest will be closed again, the ribs wired shut, the muscles stitched together, the skin sewn tight.

He speaks to me next. I know what he is thinking before he asks: where is Henry's family waiting? He must go tell them now and I will go with him. We will get the transplant nurse, though she is likely to be with the family anyway. The three of us will be in the room with the family, but he will do all the talking.

We walk slowly together down the hallways of the OR toward the family waiting room. I ask him a few questions, trying to get the facts straight in my head so that I can be clear to the family. I do not say everything I want to say, that I am wounded and full of rage at the death of this dream. Even I, the doctor who sees all the side effects; even I, the one who has built a career sweeping up all the failed miracles; even I am shocked by the weight of what is happening. But all I can think of now is what this man beside me must feel, how his hopeful heart must be breaking, how he cannot let this show. I do not ask how he feels, because what answer would suffice? I do not say, as men sometimes do to one another, *hey, you okay?* because what answer is possible? I do not look too long into his eyes when we speak. I want to give him the courtesy I need for myself, not to look too closely at all of this now, because I need enough remove from the moment to do my job. He is brave and honest and I want to do the same. Right now, acting brave and honest will be enough.

I cannot seem to swallow, but somehow I can speak in the voice I have practiced for bad news. I have never given this kind of bad news. All my previous bad news is bad luck, the result of a test or a scan. Or my bad news is so obvious already that it hardly needs telling: your gravely ill child is going to die.

This bad news is different because it is bad news erupting in the middle of hope. I know what we will have to say in a few minutes.

In mid-flight there is no safe landing.

Henry is too sick to survive this surgery without new lungs.

Henry will never get off the ventilator. Henry will never wake up. Henry has come to the end.

He will leave the OR today and make it into the ICU, but he will not leave the ICU alive. He will die with the lungs he was born with. We may never even be able to wake him up enough to say good-bye. His good-bye this morning is all there will ever be.

The surgeon and I know without saying that all this will happen. Though we will do everything we can to prevent it, we both know we will fail. So we do not speak of it as we walk toward the waiting room.

We rarely left the bedside over the next two days. We tried everything we could think of, everything the intensive care doctors could think of, every trick and every possibility to keep this boy alive. We pleaded with the organ bank to find us another set of lungs, but we knew there would be none in time. We never left him when it might have made a difference. We were there with his parents when the ventilator was removed.

DONNA, WHO DIED TWICE

Donna was a tough woman in a ruined body, the beloved of the nurses, a hater of rules, the sort who rode in an ambulance like it was a red convertible, and I wanted her to like me, though I doubt she ever did. She was twenty-two when she died the first time, the night before her lung transplant, and about to be twenty-four when she died for the second and final time. I was there both times.

She lived an hour down the coast and still went to the small children's ward at her local hospital because the adult ward knew next to nothing about cystic fibrosis. She ruled the roost in the way that an ill young woman can when she grows up among a group of nurses. They loved her deeply and wisely, never letting her be just a sick girl in a bed. They taught her to be Our Donna, the tough one, the one who comes back, the one who can take it, the one we all love. That sort of love was why she survived a child's disease.

I never saw her come to clinic with any family other than nurses from that ward. On their days off, they drove her up to Boston and sat in the waiting room with her, came into the exam room. They eyed me in that way that let me know they were paying attention: *Make us a miracle, Doctor. We know you can do it for Our Donna.*

By the time I saw her in clinic that day, Donna hadn't been out of the hospital for more than a few days in three months, even though we were treating her with every trick in the book, every antibiotic, every new therapy, every chance for improvement, however small. She had come by ambulance straight from the ward at the other hospital, a two-hour drive on a stretcher in a noisy, bumpy transport ambulance; hospital rules wouldn't allow her to come to clinic and then go back directly to the ward unless she went by ambulance. *Another silly rule in a life of silly rules,* I think she would have said. She would miss one dose of the three IV antibiotics she had been on for the last four weeks, but it was a fine risk to take, a risk we'd allow because we had a plan for Donna: a double lung transplant.

She'd been through the transplant evaluation already, the treadmill walk and the echocardiogram, the CT scans of her diseased lungs, the measurements of her chest wall volume, the surgery to open up her sinuses, the cultures of everything (blood, sputum, urine, stool), and the bone density scans. She'd had all the visits, the nutritionist, the anesthesia team, the social worker, the nurse practitioner, the insurance coordinator, the ICU staff, the physical therapist. Everything looked bad, but not bad enough to push her off the transplant list. Her right heart ventricle was enlarged, but not so enlarged that it wouldn't be able to handle the stress of the heart lung bypass machine, or do the work of pumping blood through a new set of swollen donor lungs; her chest wall was scarred, but not so scarred that she might bleed to death while the surgeons were trying to remove her old lungs; her cultures were bad, but not too bad to be treated by the antibiotics and antifungals we had. She was small, but not so small that she would need a child-size donor.

So that day before clinic, we looked up the lung waiting list in the online registry of the Organ Procurement Agency for our region, and Donna was at the top of her blood type. We already knew she was in the top two or three, but the ones ahead of her at other hospitals had been taken off the list. We would never know why. It's likely they died waiting. We didn't plan to tell Donna that. She could have guessed. When the nurse practitioner had finished talking to Donna in the clinic room, she came into the hallway to tell me, "She knows about the list. Come get me when you're done, okay?"

I knocked on the door and pushed it open with my shoulder, worrying the germs off my fingers with friction and alcohol gel. Inside the room, pointed at an angle away from the door, Donna sat in a wheelchair, her elbows on the arms, slumped over and covered in a white blanket with the blue logo of her home hospital stamped several times across the edge. The blanket was around her like a shawl, her body swallowed by the thick white cotton. Her feet rested on the paddles of the wheelchair in blue moccasins with red-and-white beading on the top. Her thin legs were wrapped in a pair of gray sweat pants that hung like loose skin over the edges of the moccasins. A navy-blue sweatshirt with some kind of design was visible under the lower edge of her blanket. She didn't look up when I came in.

I sat down on the rolling stool. I put her chart on the desk and used my heels to roll myself over toward her. Our heads were about the same height, although she was still looking straight down. I could not tell if her eyes were open.

"Hi there, Donna. Glad to see you," I said, softening my tone down to a near whisper, taking all the snap out of my voice.

She nodded.

"Feeling pretty bad, I guess." I said, still softly. "Are you any better since a few weeks ago?"

She turned her head slightly from side to side, still looking down, still bent over in the jaws of the wheelchair, and mouthed *no better*. The thin gold bracelet on her left arm trembled.

"Okay, well, I'm just going to take a listen; stay just like you are, okay."

I stood up and placed my stethoscope as softly as I could on the blanket on her back, just on the top of her chest, and listened to a breath or two on one side and then the other. All I heard were crackles, gurgling noises, and high, tight wheezes. Donna didn't take a big breath, and I didn't ask her to. No use in making her cough. Her chest shook with each breath; she was panting but doing it quietly, holding herself as still as she could, worn out and wary of a small exertion. There wasn't really any point in listening to her chest. What could I possibly hear that would make her better? But it's the routine: the lung doctor listens to your lungs, and I was thinking of what to say, stalling and imagining how Donna was feeling.

"Okay, thanks," I said, sitting back on the stool. I scooted near her, so she could hear me.

"Donna, you know about where you are on the list, right? You're next. We don't know when the call will come, but it could come tonight or next week or the week after that. We just don't know. You've got the beeper, but we'll just call the ward if we have the lungs. You'll come down here and get settled in the ICU and wait there for the OR to be ready. You know all this already, I bet."

Another nod.

"Donna, the lungs will come if you can just hang in there. You are tough and strong. I admire how tough you are, always have. Remember how you told me 'fuck off' when I wanted to listen to you in clinic a few weeks ago? Remember that?"

I laughed a small laugh, and I think Donna's head moved up and down.

"That's the strength you need now, Donna. You already have it."

I felt my voice starting to tremble. Better stop soon.

"Donna, I know you're gonna make it. Hang in there."

And she raised her head, slowly, as if it were an effort to stack her vertebra into alignment, as if she were going to take a big breath. But she didn't; she just raised her head and face toward me, looked me in the eyes, and mouthed *okay*. A whisper came out as she moved her lips, and it hung in the air between us, something more solid than all my fumbling words.

She slowly lowered her head back down and closed her eyes. I left the room to get the nurse practitioner.

Three nights later we got the call. Donna came up from the South Shore, this time with sirens blasting. The donor lungs, with their own set of sirens, came from somewhere in New England, I don't remember where, because I didn't really care. I had no room for thinking about the death of anyone but Donna; the surgeon would take care of the donor. My job was to get Donna to the OR alive.

When the EMTs rolled her stretcher into the ICU, I thought she wouldn't make it even that far. She was blue in the face, already on as much oxygen as we could give her, sweaty and pale and hypotensive, panting so hard she was not able to get even one word out. She was barely conscious, and I wasn't sure she knew where she was or who we were; she could not cooperate with any of our requests; she was rag-doll limp. She didn't have the strength to cough, and so her lungs were filling up, blocking themselves off with the cement of infected mucous that antibiotics could not kill and she could not cough out. She was about to run out of lung.

The ICU nurses went into overdrive, along with the transplant nurse practitioner. I agreed with every treatment anyone thought of, any strategy to buy time. I was trying to think of everything: a BiPAP mask, a transfusion, more nebulized antibiotics, a steroid pulse, intubation in the ICU even before the OR—we thought out loud about every possibility. And whatever we did must have worked, because she made it to the OR alive enough for the operation to start, though looking back now, I don't know why or how she survived those few hours. It wasn't anything I did.

I followed her into the operating room, too scared to leave her alone, though I had no real function there; I am not the surgeon, not the one who makes the real difference. I am not the one who can fix the problem. Donna made it onto the anesthesiologist's ventilator, survived the insertion of the epidural catheter in her back, survived while the surgeon cut the horizontal line across her chest just under her breasts—they call it a "clamshell" incision, because it opens the chest up like a mollusk—survived the insertion of the catheters into her heart for the heart-lung bypass machine, survived each and every challenge. She just kept on living in that suspended state, riding on with the help of the machines and experts, giving us just enough of a delay to do the next thing.

I see now that Donna died that night for the first time. If we hadn't had the option of the transplant exactly when we had it, almost down to the minute, she would not have made it to morning, no matter what we did, no matter where she was. I don't mean that she was "born again" with the transplant, although you could say that if you wanted to; I mean that in the hours between the time when she arrived in the ICU and the time the new lungs were put in place, Donna was in that transit zone between life and death, the limbo land of the negotiated death, when the outcome is certain but it hasn't quite happened.

She was quickly moving toward the inevitable, and we held her in our palms like water we scooped out of a fading puddle; as long as we stayed focused on keeping our hands perfectly cupped, she was safe. But you can't do that for long—the drops of water squeeze through your tight fingers, your skin absorbs the moisture, the fluid evaporates into the dry air. It should have been the last night of her life, it *was* the last night, but luck and the lottery of someone else dying nearby in just the right way and at just the right time intervened, so she survived.

Eight months later, Donna didn't show up for clinic. She didn't answer her phone. Lots of people miss clinic appointments, but not lung-transplant patients, not without calling. We were worried, though not too much.

Donna had done well. After some rough times in the intensive care unit after the transplant, she had slowly stabilized. She had some kidney damage from the immunosuppressant medication, and a host of other smaller problems, some unique to her (an infected toe, a stomach blockage, headaches, odd sinus trouble), and some typical in a patient with CF who has a lung transplant (some mild rejection on lung biopsy, thrush from the steroids, gyrating drug levels, a line infection). Nothing we couldn't handle, but she had to come to clinic. Where was she?

One week later she showed up in clinic, with a big smile on her face and a new haircut. She had flown to Las Vegas, she announced. She hadn't told us, because of course we would have said no.

She had won some money and lost some money. She had seen two shows. And she had lounged poolside at the fanciest hotel she had ever seen. She came in just to show us the pictures.

In one photo, a four-by-six-inch print, Donna reclined on a white plastic deck chair, the kind with two- or three-inch straps across the back. The sky above her was a hard blue, and there were no shadows. A green palm sat behind her chair in a waist-high terra cotta planter with a scalloped rim. A small round, glass-topped table was arranged on her left side, with magazines and a Walkman on it, the dark-blue headphone cords dangled over the edge of the table. Donna wore one of those lady-golfer, open-topped visor hats with her ponytail tied high and tight off the back of her head. The part in her shiny blond-brown hair showed over the top of the visor. She held a foot-tall glass, dripping with frost and crowned by a small umbrella and a straw, filled with pink liquid and ice cubes.

"A Vegas Whopper, they called it—really good!" she said, dancing lightly over the fact that she was forbidden to drink alcohol when on her transplant meds.

"Oh, Donna!" and "Don-na!" we all said, with no real exasperation. "Just what did you think you were up to?"

"You didn't notice the best part," she said, smiling. "Look closer!"

And so we all looked.

I didn't see anything else and passed the photo back to the nurse practitioner, who looked at the picture again and said, "What is it, sweetheart?"

"It's the bikini, you dummies! You can't see my transplant scar! I had to shop for weeks to find it!"

And then Donna laughed without coughing one bit.

A year after the transplant, the complications began to pile up: More renal problems and more gyrations in the immunosuppressant levels, rejection on the lung biopsies followed by big blasts of steroids to try to stop the rejection, followed by the development of diabetes and the need for insulin; intestinal blockage, again; a broken pelvis from the brittle bones caused by the steroids needed to control the rejection. Pain from the broken bones and the scars that made getting out of bed a chore again. The worst was more breathlessness, more cough and wheeze as the new lungs fought against the immune system of the old body. Donna's chest X-rays went from the beautiful dark black of a clean lung to the flurry of scarring and rejection to the white canvas of nonfunctional lungs. She had to go back on extra oxygen. Her pulmonary function tests fell from their happy post-transplant heights, numbers Donna had not reached since she was a small child. Her lungs were back at the levels before the transplant.

We began to do more of the visits over the phone, or sometimes the nurse practitioner drove down to see her, meeting Donna at her apartment with one of the nurses from South Shore. The circle of nurses gathered around her again and called us with worry in their voices at first, but then they stopped calling because they knew what our answers were going to be.

The week before Donna died for the second time, she was admitted to our transplant ward. We were hoping that we could just patch her up enough to go home again, though we knew the end was near. When I saw her arrive in the ward, again in an ambulance, I knew this would be the last time. Donna's heart was failing, her kidneys were close to complete collapse, she needed oxygen around the clock, and the carbon dioxide was building up in her blood, a sign that her lungs were unable to get out the burned-up fumes of the body's furnace. Three days later we moved her to the ICU, to a glass-walled room in the back corner across from the nursing desk, and we told everyone to come say good-bye.

Donna drifted in and out for two days, gaining and losing consciousness as the carbon dioxide levels floated up and down. She stopped making any urine because her kidneys could not function; her low blood pressure was controlled only because of the adrenaline drips running into her body through two separate IV lines.

I couldn't stay out of her room. I had to be there, or waiting just outside, or at the desk, but close-by. I had other patients in the hospital, and other phone calls, and I hurried through all of them so I could get back to the ICU. At morning rounds with the transplant team, the transplant surgeon seemed relieved that I was taking charge. He didn't want to be there, and he was glad to hand things over to me when death was near; that was how we worked together, and I was grateful to him for this understanding. One of the surgical interns, a young man in his first months as a doctor, asked about an experimental blood-filtration process that Donna could have at the hospital across town. The transplant surgeon looked at him with open irritation, something I had never seen him do in years of working together.

"Her limbs are cold on full pressors. Her CO2 is through the roof. Her lungs are full of scarring. She's had enough. We are not going anywhere."

The intern said, "But what about . . ." and his voice trailed off as the surgeon turned to face me. We are friends, I think, and we know what things are hard for each of us to do.

The surgeon said, "Walter, call me."

"I will. I will."

He moved on with his team, on to the next sick child who needed saving, on to the child only he could heal. I stayed with Donna.

I remember the events of that day always in the present tense. I cannot be sure that the way it happens in my memory is the way it happened then. I can report what happened in the way a doctor's note reports it, full of lab values, oxygen levels, therapies added and subtracted; I can still do that, because it is my medical habit, and that habit dies hard. That report would tell one version of the truth, a conflation of the past and the present fixed in medical jargon and suitable for viewing in some public tribunal.

But listen to me, you families who read this—the world of the dying happens outside that simple focus of medicine. Every moment here has more than one meaning. Time accelerates and then slows, and the sequence is not fixed.

Our actions echo through memory, forward and backward, becoming turning points for us but then regressing out of focus. What we capture in memory is sharpened by our tumbling thoughts, the force of memory smoothing the edges, shearing off the details.

Listen to me: A clinical report will not do here. It will not do for Donna. It will no longer do for me.

Donna's ICU bed is cranked up to the level of the elbows of the people caring for her. This makes it easier to get at the tubes and wires and equipment. It also gets the patient's face closer to ours, so we can whisper and talk, when there is still the ability to talk. We all want to be close. Donna's head is propped up by one or two firm pillows, her forehead is beaded with moisture, and her damp hair is pushed over the top of her head and draped thinly across the pillowcase. Her mouth is slack, her lower lip tucked over to the right in a limp wrinkle. I can see her teeth in the shadows of her dry mouth, and her tongue is cracked and pink. Her lips are blue, a color we call *dusky* for its unnaturalness; living lips are supposed to be pink or red, not this matte indigo.

Her chest is covered in a hospital gown, because we have run out of the clothes she brought from home and she hasn't been awake enough to complain about the scratchy gowns. There is a clean white sheet drawn up to her lower chest. The top edge of the sheet rests about where her transplant scar is, now fully healed, a quarter-inch-thick line dotted by the small pinpricks of the staples that closed the final layer of skin. She has eight other scars on her torso that I knew of: six from the post-op chest tubes, one from her gastrostomy tube, and one from the exploratory surgery on her belly, the second time she had a bowel obstruction, nine months ago now. She has a urinary catheter going into her bladder, but the blue-and-clear plastic bag hanging off the side of the bedrail is empty; she has not made much urine for a few days, and like the carbon dioxide her lungs could not exhale, the toxins in her blood still circulate, since her kidneys can no longer filter them out.

But she is still breathing. The receptors in her brain that signal when to breathe still work, though they fire erratically. She takes sharp inward breaths, twelve times a minute, as if surprised by a ghost before every breath, and her chest drops quickly down at the end of the breath. She is not making any gurgling sounds in her mouth or in the back of her throat because we have positioned her head so that her throat hangs open in just the right way; there is no longer any muscle tone holding her throat open, and in any other position she would have been sending out waves of noise with each breath. A clear-plastic, half-circular mask about the size of a baseball mitt cups her chin and blows oxygen and mist into the open space in front of her mouth. A blue crinkled tube connects to the mask just at the level of the chin, giving the impression, from a distance, of a pale-blue King Tut chin beard that trails down between her covered breasts. The tube takes a left turn over the side of the bed and ends in a bubbling plastic bottle of humidifying saline plugged into the oxygen valve in the wall.

Throughout morning and night, Donna slips away, out of our gathered hands and into unconsciousness, as her breath slows and slows in irregular waves. Soon there is nothing but those surprised soundless gasps, as if she has suddenly been called back toward the living borderland and remembers that she must breathe as long as she stays. But then minutes pass between breaths. The monitor shows a dim-green wave, the electrical activity of the dying heart, twitching and firing without pumping blood.

The sun sets so gradually inside her face. Pink and blue becomes gray and then white so softly, the hush and hang of an unsounded note.

I went to the funeral at the Catholic church in her South Shore town. It was a blustery day, cold enough to expect snow. I was squinting to keep the frozen street grit of the New England winter out of my eyes, but I saw the transplant nurse practitioner on the church steps and we went in to sit together in the back.

The church was full enough. A young woman who lives her life in hospitals does not have classmates and coworkers to come to her funeral. There were hothouse flowers on the altar, and the casket was down front in the nave, and if I craned my neck to the right I could get a glimpse of polished brown wood through the shoulders of the mourners. The service started; maybe there were relatives who read some parts of the service; maybe there were hymns sung without a choir to the accompaniment of wheezing organ; I can't separate the details from all the other funerals. I was present but lost inside my thoughts.

My goal was to be at the periphery of grief. When I was a young doctor, I imagined that my presence at a funeral might offer some solace, but it doesn't. The doctor is a smaller part of living and dying than people imagine. We are not the central character in the story. I came here for the reason anyone goes to a funeral—I want to join with others in acknowledging the importance of Donna's life to me, but I don't want to intrude.

The priest, a man in his mid-sixties with thick white hair, was standing in the pulpit on the high left side of the church; his vestment, an ecru robe with embroidery too fine for me to see clearly, swung around his paunch as he climbed the narrow staircase up to the pulpit. I was distractedly thinking now of Donna, then about another patient back at the hospital, then about myself, until I realized that the reading and the homily were on the story of Lazarus.

Yes, he's talking about Lazarus, I thought, how Jesus so loved Lazarus that he raised him up, resurrected his body with a touch and a call to *Arise, Beloved one*. This priest, a man in a cassock who never knew her— I can't imagine Donna was the churchgoing sort—is telling her assembled family that Jesus so loved a man that He called upon a days-dead body to arise and walk, and the priest is saying all this ten feet in the air above Donna's lifeless body, held still and dark inside that box. This man is talking about how much the Father-and-Son Rulers of the Universe loved someone else enough to bring him back to his family, back to the world of the breathing. The priest is saying that love can make some people's death an illusion, that faith brings resurrection. But the presence of the gleaming casket finishes his sentence for him—faith brought life to Lazarus but not to Our Donna.

Anger flooded my throat.

I wanted to shout—let there be no talk of Lazarus here!

Do not say that our faith was not enough. Donna, the woman you never knew, was resurrected, and it was an against-the-odds Las Vegas miracle of luck and faith enough for an entire crowd. That it didn't last was not for lack of love.

I wanted to shout away his memorized phrases, bring a moment of life into the last time all of us who knew Donna will gather. I wanted to offer up my own evidence of the ways of living and dying.

But all I did was weep, my throat clenched in anger and sorrow.

But now I can write my own liturgy for her and for myself, the words I would have said were I in charge of our grief.

Here is what this doctor knows: I am the black box of this death, burned and buried in a field of debris, ready to reveal the details of the crash.

Gathered friends, loving nurses, grieving family, hear me. Your child, your friend, your tough-as-nails darling, your beloved Donna, let her live and die and live again in your memory. Let her story mean something more than the failure of faith or love. Let her be her own miracle.

THE NECESSARY MONSTER

1.

The young boy knew what all children know: there is a monster in the dark space under the bed, invisible in daylight but all too real at night, and it unfolds from its lair a half hour or so before bedtime. It hisses through pointed teeth, its yellow eyes blinking with sideways lids and its talons ragged and ready to grab the ankle of any boy foolish enough not to fear it. The boy would leap into the bed from three feet away so that the gnarled arms could not catch him, and once in bed he would stay in the absolute middle of the mattress, arms tucked under the covers and hands brought in tight against his chest. The terror was real enough to make him wheeze, and so to stop the high-pitched sound of his breathing—surely the siren song for reptilian ears—he would practice blowing out through pursed lips and drawing in breath through his nose. The underbed monster would at first be content to pinch off a careless toe or finger left too near the edge of the bed, but as the moments passed the beast would need to feed itself on a more delicious meal, his escalating dread. The monster's fear-gathering method was simple: fill up the silences of the night with creaking and knocking noises that anyone who didn't know better would think were just the sounds of the old house settling. Monsters under the bed know how a boy's fear works.

The boy could not, as his father told him to do, just look under the bed to prove there was no monster. He could not, as his mother instructed, just stop being so sensitive. He had to learn to provide his own comfort in the middle of the night. So he invented new monsters that would challenge the beast under the bed, horrible monsters that would claw and snarl just enough to distract the gruesome thing underneath him until morning. These invented monsters were necessary to his survival. They varied from night to night. Some nights there was one crouching silently behind the shoes at the back of the closet. Other nights there was one who exhaled steam from behind the radiator. On windy nights, a necessary monster lurked on the window ledge in the hairy darkness outside, watching through the panes, tapping on the glass with its tree-limb arms and leafy scales. The closet and radiator and window-ledge monsters raged against every living thing, as monsters must, but they reserved their special hatred for the terrible emperor of the underbed world. These necessary monsters were the protectors a boy needs to survive.

Monster warfare would begin when he was in bed with his eyes shut. Every sound, every rumble or shake, the rattle of a window frame, every scratch or creak was a signal that the monsters were beginning their terrible ritual. There was no need to watch their brutal struggles, and anyway he could not really see them if he did open his eyes, for everyone knew that monsters were experts at hiding in the slanting shadows and weak moonlight. And if he did look, the glint reflected in his eyes might distract the protecting monsters from the danger under the bed; then his rescuers might decide to snatch him up for themselves. But if he stayed still with his eyes closed, the necessary monsters would ignore him. After all, he ruled no kingdom, he held no treasure; he wasn't much of a morsel to a serious monster. Ravaging him would give no glory. Real glory would come in defeating the terrible underbed beast by punching its gnashing teeth, slapping its warty lips, and then flinging it back into the recesses of folded space beneath the bed.

The boy knew it was foolish not to believe in the monster under the bed. That he couldn't convince his parents of this terrible reality was confusing, but he didn't need to convince them once he had the protection of the other monsters. As long as the helpful monsters could keep an uneasy peace, he could slip unnoticed between the cool sheets and descend into the quiet of sleep for another night, where he felt safe, or safe enough.

By morning, everything was fine again. Everyone, even six-year-olds, knows that monsters hate the daylight.

That summer the boy's mother announced that he was going to eat a peanut butter and jelly sandwich for lunch every day for a week, starting on Monday. She had been considering this plan for some time, telling him that his previous reaction to peanuts was a made-up thing:

"For heaven's sake, son, you can be allergic to a flower, but you can't be allergic to a sandwich! I've never heard of such a thing."

"You're not 'allergic,' you just don't like it because one time you ate a piece of the peanut shell by accident."

"No one will invite a child over to play if he refuses to eat what the mother makes for lunch."

"A boy who won't eat peanut butter will have no friends at all."

His mother was not going to raise a rude and friendless child. So he sat at the table each day, eating one bite of the peanut butter sandwich, in tears, lips and throat burning, wheezing and scratching before running to the bathroom and vomiting the bite right back up. And the rest of the day he lay on the sofa trying to recover, not daring to turn on the TV lest his mother think he was faking. He went to bed early and wallowed in his fears of the thing under the bed, glad for the quiet of a familiar fright.

By lunchtime the next day the rash had vanished and he wasn't wheezing and it seemed to his mother that nothing had really happened anyway, so they started over again. Day after day, he took one bite through tears, and then the rash and the itch and the wheezing and the vomiting would overwhelm him. The boy didn't really know what an allergy was, of course. He didn't know why his head screamed not to eat the sandwich, why his stomach ached and the crooks of his arms itched whenever he smelled peanut butter. He had no idea what was going on, and he didn't even have the presence of mind—what six-year-old does?—to think any of this through. Here's what he knew: His mother was always right. He was bad. He wanted to be good. So every day he took the bite of sandwich. By Thursday she relented, tired of the whole thing, and likely disappointed with her foolish son who could not learn to act right and who might never have any friends.

Two years later his mother took him for allergy testing because he started to need asthma medication every day. Asthma was a diagnosis a mother could believe.

Once he was in the allergist's examination room, the nurse dressed him in a scratchy blue shirt with the back open and the sleeves rolled up. She had a nurse's cap on, an architectural marvel, so stiff, so white, so much like a crown that it made her seem more official and serious, like the nurses on TV. (Mrs. Williams, the nurse at the pediatrician's office, wore a white dress with blue stripes on the sleeves, but she had nothing on her head at all. She could have been anybody.)

Next the nurse drew a series of boxes in blue ink on the inside of both his forearms and in two rows down his bare back. Drawing the boxes on his back felt like that game he played with his older sisters, when one of them would draw out a word on his back with her finger and get him to guess the word, *dog* or *jump* or *bark* or the hardest one, *pajamas*. The nurse had a tray of clear glass vials with black caps, each one numbered in white, and each one at least half full of liquid. She opened them to reveal a small stick inside each cap and told him to hold as still as he could. She used the little sticks to scratch his arms and back inside the blue boxes. The little spikes in the caps were coated, he knows now, in different allergens, trees and bushes and grasses and dust mites and eggs and milk. And peanuts.

After the testing was over, the doctor came in and sat on the rolling silver stool they always seem to have. The boy can remember now what the doctor said, or something very much like it.

"The tests are pretty clear, Mrs. Robinson. You must already know he is very allergic to peanuts, right? Allergic to all nuts. And for the rest, it's not too bad, just trees and grasses, just standard hay fever, and we can set up some shots for that without a problem. Your pediatrician can give the shots; I'll figure out the doses. But no peanuts, of course; in fact no nuts at all."

The boy and his mother never went back to that allergist. There were no more peanut butter sandwiches on his plate, but that didn't mean his mother stopped having peanut butter in the house or stopped putting almonds in the green beans at Thanksgiving or stopped adding pecans in the sweet potatoes on New Year's Day. She didn't stop putting peanut candy in his Christmas stocking. His father kept eating peanuts by the handful with his can of beer at night. The boy learned to ask what was in the food in a quiet voice, off to the side, or to explore the kitchen for signs of nuts that might have been added to casseroles or stews so he could avoid them at the table. If he asked whether there were nuts in some dish, the answer was, *Oh, honey, I'm not sure, can't you just pick them out?* and the subject was changed. He learned to leave things untouched on the plate.

The mother and son did not discuss nuts or allergies again until a visit home when he was fifty-one and she was eighty-six. It didn't surprise him that it took that long, accustomed as he was to all the things his parents preferred not to discuss. Out of the blue while they were sitting at the breakfast room table, she brought up feeding him those sandwiches. She recounted it as a funny sort of story a mother tells about her inexperience, like turning the shirts pink in the washer or a badly done home haircut. He laughed along with her, never telling her how he had dined out for years on the story of "Sandwich Week," as he had come to call it, with friends and strangers alike gasping in amazement at his mother's child-rearing strategies. People would tell him how mad the story made them, how they just couldn't believe how some mothers can do such monstrous things to their children. Sometimes when he told this story, especially after he first left home, he would let the point of his story be that his mother was some sort of monster, an unfeeling woman who put her fears about herself ahead of her son's welfare.

But as the years went by he softened the story, or tried to, making his mother seem well intentioned but mistaken. After all, she didn't want to hurt her son. She wanted to protect him. She was doing what she saw as her job, defending him against the friendless future she feared for him. His differences—the nut allergy, being "too sensitive," not having enough friends, not going on dates, not marrying, moving away from his home town, and so many others—were to her all signs of weakness, and weakness had to be pruned before it took root. Sandwich Week was just the first battle in a much longer war over the sort of person her son would be allowed to become.

What he didn't say when he entertained people with the story of Sandwich Week was that for most of his life, he thought his mother was right: he *was* too sensitive and too awkward and too bookish; he *was* uncomfortable with people and easily embarrassed; he *was* someone quite different with people and alone, and the erasure of his nature was both his inheritance and his private daily struggle. He wished he could just eat what was offered him, take part in what life put on his plate, but something in him always made that sort of life impossible. He couldn't shake the sense that he was damaged beyond rescue. People thought his mother was monstrous, but he knew better: she was a monster of necessity who fought the dangers she could see in order to protect her child from a more terrible fate. Some monsters are on our side.

2.

The boy grew up to be a medical student, and he met his first gay man with AIDS on the ninth floor of Grady Hospital in 1985 As the third-year student on the internal medicine rotation, he had to check on all the patients on his list, though the student did not know why exactly the man was in the hospital. Everyone went into the rooms of people with HTLV-3, as the virus was called then, dressed as though nearness could kill. For all the student knew, it might. Yellow gowns, clear gloves, and blue masks were stacked in boxes outside the room on the plastic handrails that the other patients used to walk along the hospital floors, and their presence outside the room instead of inside was meant to signal the elevated danger inside the room—this unseen thing behind the door was dangerous. Usually the red clipboard with the vital signs hung on that railing as well, but even that was absent. But this man was on the list, and the student had to go in. He did not realize it at the time, but what he feared more than any virus was that the patient would recognize him as another gay man.

The student wrapped a yellow gown over his short white coat and put a mask over his mouth and nose and gloves on his hands. He knocked on the door and walked inside to be stunned by the reeking, stale, smoky, barren room—certainly not like any hospital room he had been in so far, though all the hospital rooms stank of something. But this stink was new. The student knew the staff was vigilant about the other patients not being allowed to smoke, especially the COPD patients he had learned to call "chronic lungers" and the veterans with heart disease who told him to "fuck off, sonny" when he asked them not to smoke with their oxygen tanks, but there this man sat, in a haze of smoke on a narrow hospital bed, the sheets rumpled and half on the floor and the dun-colored tray usually used for vomit sitting on the bedside table full of used butts. A silver Zippo lighter sat next to a pack of Kools on the table. Maybe the nurses let this patient smoke because it was the only comfort they had to offer, or maybe they never went into the room enough to argue with him. The patient had a dyed-blond buzz cut and blond stubble with collapsed cheeks. He was dressed in a thin white undershirt, his own, no hospital gown. A large bore IV ran into one arm and another one dove under his shirt to his chest, or so the student imagined, since he would never get close enough to this patient to examine him.

The student said, "Hello, Mr. --, I'm a medical student here to check how you are doing this morning," and the patient said, "Yeah, sure," in a strong Georgia accent with no hint of softness and only a bit of patience, his eyes never leaving the TV screen on the wall. "Any pain last night? How'd you sleep? Anything you need from us today?" The student asked all three questions in a hurry; the room was choking him, and they both knew there wasn't anything the student could do about pains or sleep.

The student took the red clipboard off the bottom of the bed and looked at the chart of vitals, trying to memorize them since his notebook and pen were in his coat under the gown, and he didn't want to touch anything in the room. He looked at the patient's yellow-grey skin—he should have known this was jaundice from liver disease, but at the time he was more filled with fear than reason—and surveyed the wasted arm muscles and thin neck, seemingly too thin to hold up a man's head. A thought crossed the student's mind: the body is dead yet the person lives on. He tried not to show any reaction to this thought, though the patient could not have seen the student's face behind the mask.

The yellowing man paused after the barrage of questions, and then said, "Ah, nothin', same as usual," his voiced rising on *saym* and falling into a slurred finish with *use-yull*. The student wanted to cut him off and get out of there before he revealed any of his real problems, so he said, "Okay, then, thanks," and ripped off the yellow gown and the mask and turned his gloves inside out to throw them in the full trash can next to the door. He never turned around to say good-bye. He got out into the hallway and washed his hands in a sink nearby, wondering if the smell of the cigarettes would stick to him for the rest of the day.

Later, the medial team stood outside their patient's door, discussing his lab values but not his prognosis or plan. No one asked the student anything. As they finished, the attending said, "Well, no need to disturb him this morning," though every other patient was disturbed by the medical team's leisure multiple times per day. The student joined in the barely concealed disgust the doctors had for the man. No part of him wanted to object to this casual hatred of a sick man lest his speaking up would smear him with the same hatred. He told himself he had nothing to do with this patient's illness, nothing at all. His loosened his jaw and tried to give his own face the same look as the senior doctors, betraying nothing of himself and hoping they did not see the blush of shame and fear on his face. The next day the man was not on the student's list to check, and the student did not think of him until about a week later, when he wondered where the man had gone. He doesn't even remember the man's name.

A month or so later, the student was "invited to assist" with a colonoscopy at the pediatric hospital. The invitation was not a measure of hospitality. Being "invited to assist" was code that a medical student needed to hold something out of the way, like an organ or roll of fat, so the real doctor could do real work, undisturbed and with a better view.

A typical procedure in the operating room went like this: the student stood back from the body with his gloved hand holding a retractor on something, perhaps the liver edge, with just the right amount of tension so that the surgeon could get a good look at something else, such as the head of the pancreas. The "right" amount of tension was a term of art—not so little that the field of view was obstructed and not so much that the liver was bruised. Doing this right was impossible since he couldn't see the liver edge because of the more important people blocking his view. But it did not matter. He soldiered on in spite of the likely failure. Like a Foreign Legion recruit, he was proud to be present in the war on disease, even though his presence would put his flaws on display. He offered himself up for the use of his betters. For the medical student, being a living armature for a surgeon was the closest he had come to practicing medicine. So when he was "invited to assist," there was no question of declining.

Two years prior to that invitation, during the third month of medical school, an adult gastrointestinal (GI) doctor came to anatomy class to show colonoscopy videos. After first showing a film of the camera moving along the intestine—the student could only think of those filmed tunnel rides with the camera at the front of a subway train—the GI doctor brought out his endoscope from its special metal briefcase and held up in his hands like an impossibly long snake with matte-black skin and a metal mouth. How could that thing fit inside a body? A mischievous student, perhaps a second-year, had spread the rumor that this doctor liked to demonstrate the camera on medical students. The young man was convinced he might be called on at any minute to pull down his pants and show the entire class his innards. Of course, the GI doctor did not "demonstrate" on any one. The young man ought to have guessed this, so commonplace was this sort of rumor in the hazing atmosphere of medical school. His habit in that first year was to anticipate embarrassment without stopping to calculate its likelihood, and he was so beset with worry about being called upon that he didn't absorb the content of the lecture. So here he was at his first colonoscopy not knowing what to expect (other than some version of the subway-tunnel film) and too embarrassed to reveal his ignorance.

On arriving at the endoscopy suite, the student was quickly briefed by the attending doctor: the patient was a ten-year-old boy with short gut syndrome caused by an abdominal "stroke" in the neonatal intensive care unit, necessitating the removal of a large portion of his intestines. The boy was here for a routine colonoscopy with biopsies. The whole thing was no big deal.

The boy had been partly sedated. His eyes were open in a blank stare and his thin blond hair was stuck against his forehead with sweat. He was on his right side on a short gurney with the lower half of his body covered by a half sheet. He had socks on, the kind a pediatric hospital provides with traction strips sewn into the soles so the kids don't slip in the hallways. His thin arms stuck out of a blue hospital gown decorated with dancing panda bears.

From his vantage point at the head of the bed, the medical student could not see the tube go into the boy's rectum. He looked at the screen that showed the camera image of the boy's insides, though he had no real idea what he was seeing. The boy began to squirm, and then it became clear to the student why he had been invited: he was the child-restraint system for this procedure. He bent over the edge of the stretcher and reached down to hold the boy's hands and arms. The boy twisted in the student's grip and began to moan with a varying tone, sometimes starting low and escalating up the scale to a squeal, followed by short gasping sounds and then a medium-voiced moan bent in the middle, a sharp spike followed by a return to mid-voice. Then the boy began to pull his legs up so that, to keep him still, the student had to brace one forearm across the boy's upper body and hold the boy's knees down with the other arm, bending over the child's body like a wrestler.

And then the boy got louder, not screaming, but loud enough to be heard through the door. He began to say half phrases like "lemme 'lone!" and "no-don'!" all in the half-asleep voice a child uses to escape from a goblin in a nightmare. His body writhed to get away from the foot of the bed, and the doctor said sharply, "Hold him still." And then, "Hold him, now!" The boy's face would relax for a moment and then twist back again into that terrible grimace, the face of a half-aware child in a nightmare. The student began to whisper to the boy *it's all okay, it's all right, it's all okay, you're okay* in a low voice so that the attending and nurse might not hear. He didn't know what to say, but he could not be silent. He knew in that moment that he was more afraid of displeasing the doctor than of causing the boy pain, but he viewed the boy's squirming as evidence of his lack of skill at restraining him. The doctor kept saying, "Hold him still, hold him still," and the student gripped the boy's arms so tightly that sweat began to drip down the back of his starched white shirt. The room was whirring with the sound of the fans on the computers and screens. The student was trying to look at the screen, not because he understood what he saw but because he wanted to imagine that something would be found to justify this brutality. With every one of the boy's protests, the student's mind rang out in anger, "Stop it! Can't you see you are hurting him?" But he said nothing.

Then the scope was removed, and the boy stopped squirming, and the lights were turned on, and the student repositioned the boy's body back on the stretcher, sideways and curled up on the narrow bed. The student stepped back and wiped the sweat off his forehead as he took off his yellow gown. Mumbling something about having to get to a lecture, he walked through the swinging doors and into the hallway, shaking with rage at the doctor and furious with himself for his silent collaboration.

The day after the colonoscopy, the nurse from the GI suite came up to the medical student to say, "I could see you were upset by the procedure yesterday, but he was just uncomfortable from the air pumped into the intestine to give the surgeon a good look—that doesn't really hurt. We know this kiddo; he's had this procedure lots of times before. And you should know that the kid does not remember any of that—the Versed gives them amnesia. Don't they teach you that? Whatever happens in the room, they cannot remember it once it is over. And it's all for his own good."

So, he thought as she talked, *it's all okay because his pain was not real pain? Because we have done it to him before? Because doing it that way is better for the doctor? Because the drugs mean the boy won't remember it? Because it's all for his own good?*

The student smiled and thanked her for speaking with him. He knew enough not to contradict the nurse. He hoped his face did not betray his thoughts. He cleared his mind and got back to work.

3.

The medical student became an intern whose days were filled with sick children and broken families: micro-preemies with HIV and wounded addict mothers, children poisoned by flecks of lead paint on the crumbling walls of the only apartments their parents could afford, babies born with congenital syphilis screaming to be held through thick walls of quarantining plastic; these were children who had problems no superhero could begin to vanquish, much less a young doctor six months after receiving his diploma.

One afternoon he was called to the ER as part of the pediatric surgical team. Though he was in training to be a pediatrician, one of his monthly rotations was on the surgical service. The older pediatricians told the intern he was on the surgical team to protect the children from the surgeons; the older surgeons told him he was on the surgical team to learn to be useful for a change.

The intern entered the treatment room of the pediatric ER to find a twelve-year-old boy sitting uncomfortably on a stretcher. The boy did not seem to be in pain. His cheeks were red in the way that pubescent boys' cheeks sometimes are as the flush of hormones takes hold, and he wore a too-large T-shirt with some writing on it that the intern did not recognize. The boy's legs and feet hung over the small stretcher, and he swung them back and forth in the impatient way of boys of his age. The senior surgical resident, using the sort of voice adults use to explain things to children, stood in the middle of the treatment room and announced to both the intern and the boy, "This is Michael. He has a chest wall abscess. We are going to take care of it for him." Michael did not flinch at or show concern over this plan, though he hardly looked relieved or reassured. The intern decided to copy Michael's approach, as he had never seen an abscess in the chest wall before today, much less drained one, and he possessed only a vague idea about the specifics. He had, however, been a doctor long enough to know not to show his ignorance.

The surgical resident helped Michael take off his shirt and told him to lie down on the stretcher. He put on sterile gloves and washed the skin of Michael's right upper chest with soap and water, starting in the center and working outward in a spiral motion. He changed his gloves and then used a sponge soaked in Betadine, the oily antiseptic that leaves a stain like an old bruise, to draw the same sort of spiral on the boy's chest, widening the area as he went, creating a sterile area about four inches outward from a quarter-sized red and swollen spot on Michael's skin. The intern hadn't noticed the swollen spot until the resident started to clean the skin over it: there was no break in the skin, no obvious injury or bruising to the chest wall. The intern would learn later that a chest wall abscess doesn't need an entry wound, and that it is diagnosed more by feel than sight: the fluid underneath the swollen area makes the skin warm to the touch, and the right sort of touch would reveal the sensation of thick fluid moving beneath the skin and fat. The medical term for that feeling under the fingers was *fluctuance*. In this case the fluid was outside the muscles of the ribs but underneath the skin and subcutaneous fat. The intern could picture the anatomy in his head. *The fluid has to come out*, he thought, *because an abscess has to be drained, but are we going to use a needle to suck the fluid out? A tube? An incision? What?*

In a coordinated movement that reminded the intern of a magician doing a card trick, the surgical resident draped a square of white plastic paper with a hole in the center over the red spot, turning the swelling into a target. The resident told Michael to turn his head over to the other side, away from the side of the swelling, and said, "Just relax, Michael." Then the resident turned away to the small rolling silver table at the bedside and made some rustling noises in moving the unneeded drapes around on the table. He turned back around holding a small syringe in his gloved hand. The intern knew on sight from the size of the needle that this wouldn't be used to drain the abscess. This was just lidocaine, an anesthetic used to numb the skin and the tissues just under the skin in preparation for whatever would happen next. It's the drug the intern had used before to put in stitches in the ER or a central IV in the ICU—he knew all about this. The needle is small, and the injection stings, but after a minute or so, the skin becomes numb and the patient doesn't feel the suture and thread or the large bore catheter. For those procedures, this needle was the only physical pain involved, and it was like a bee sting or a bug bite—short, sharp, and transient.

From his vantage point, Michael could not see the needle coming. One moment before the needle went in, the resident said, "Small pinch, Michael. Just hold still." As he said this, the surgeon glanced at the intern with a look he had seen many times before, and now the intern recognized his role in this procedure. In one swift move right before the needle went in, the intern used one hand to hold Michaels' head and neck in place, and the other to pin the boy's shoulder to the table. By this time in his training, the intern knew how to hold a kid down. Michael winced and said something like "aaaahhhhh!" when the needle went in, but as the skin ballooned out with the fluid being pushed in, he settled down; the anesthetic was working to numb the feeling even of the needle itself. The intern relaxed his grip but kept his hands in position in case Michael tried to move or to touch the sterile area.

While they waited for the anesthetic to numb Michael's chest wall, the surgical resident began speaking to Michael in a soothing sing-song way, saying, "The worst is over, everything will be fine, you're doing a good job," in a tone like the one the intern used every day, a whispering incantation in the voice of the lullaby-singing snake from *The Jungle Book* movie—a low, smooth rhythm of repetition that he would use to mesmerize his child victims into compliance. That voice worked better than silence, or so the intern thought—it kept the child's attention on something other than anticipation or fear. *What was his name, that snake?* he thought as they waited for the anesthetic to kick in, *Was it Kaa, or something like that? The song was called "Trust in Me," wasn't it?*

Thinking about the mesmerizing voice trick made the intern think about the idea of "the treatment room," they were in, the sort of place he hadn't seen in medical school. One of the senior pediatricians described it this way: the treatment room was a place away from the child's bed on the ward or the exam rooms of the ER where children were brought for procedures. This room was spare compared to the bright colors of the rest of the ward, and there were counters and cabinets stocked with needles, IV catheters and bags, a code cart, a defibrillator, and bandages of all sorts, as well as a narrow stretcher set up in the middle of the room like an altar. The idea was that the painful aspects of treatment shouldn't happen just anywhere, and never in the child's bed—the bed was to be a place of refuge where the child could feel safe. When you weren't in the treatment room, there wasn't supposed to be pain or fear.

The intern knew this was nonsense. No change of location was going to fool a sick child. The pain and fear of the treatment room followed the children back to their beds, and hospital beds, with their IV tubes and poles and their odd noises and strange lights and constant interruptions by strangers, were hardly places of comfort for a child. Children knew that no matter the room, no matter the location, the people in charge can hurt you and tell you it's for your own good. That this transaction occurred in a special room off to the side of the ward was a comfort only for the doctors.

The senior pediatrician had also discouraged the interns from wearing white coats. This was a surprise, as white coats were required on everyone, senior and junior, at the intern's medical school, where they were seen as an essential feature of professionalism and a mark of respect for the seriousness of the work. But during residency, the older pediatricians thought the children would come to associate the white coats with the pain the doctors caused and would be afraid every time anyone in a white coat approached them. So the interns were not to wear white coats. But the intern still stuck needles in children, and if he didn't wear a white coat then the kids might think everyone who approached them might have a needle or a scalpel. When the senior pediatricians had outlined this rule, he wondered, *Wasn't it better that the kids can see me coming and know exactly who to fear? Isn't it our job to own up to being the source of pain?* The intern had also thought, *Was it just that the senior doctors, the ones who never drew blood or put in IVs, didn't want their badge of compassion soiled with a bit of blood and pain?*

The intern now heard the surgical resident swivel toward the small table and saw him turn back toward Michael's chest with a scalpel in his gloved hand. With the index and third finger of his left hand, the surgical resident rocked the swollen lump under the skin back and forth to feel the outlines of the abscess cavity and made a one-inch incision on top of the mound, and then another one perpendicular to that, a small perfect cross on the reddened skin. Michael didn't move at all. At first only a small flash of red blood appeared at the edge of the cut, and then a single drop ran out of the end of the incision. Not satisfied, the surgical resident held the point of the scalpel perpendicular to the skin and pushed it in deeper. A burst of neon-yellow pus, thin and greasy-looking with strings of blood, flooded out of the incision and ran down to soak the edge of the white drapery. The resident held a wad of gauze in his left hand and began to press as much fluid out of the hole as he could, massaging the cavity under the skin to milk its infected contents.

Michael stayed quiet on the stretcher, with no need to hold him down.

The smell was overwhelming: both rotten and fresh; raw meat newly gone bad. It crowded the air around the intern in putrid waves. With fresh eruption of pus, the smell intensified until it seemed to the intern to cover his face and saturate his head. He held his lips tightly closed and clenched his throat. He backed away from the boy on the stretcher. He thought, *I have to get away from this.*

But as he stepped back from the stretcher, the smell seemed to come with him, clinging to his shirt, to his face. When he was forced to breathe in, the reek swam into his mouth with the air, coating his tongue. He turned to walk quickly out the door, and then he ran ten or so feet down the hallway into a small bathroom, slammed the door, and vomited once, loudly, into the toilet. A retching, expelling force pushed his throat open and out came everything until there was nothing left. His body still clenched at the smell. He flushed the toilet quickly and washed his hands, wiping his face and mouth with a wet paper towel. He paused to straighten his tie and pat down his unruly hair, but in the hard light over the mirror his face looked like a damp and rumpled bed.

Had they heard him vomit in the next room? How could they not?

He exited the bathroom and walked back into the treatment room as the resident was packing long narrow strips of gauze into the abscess cavity with a pair of curved-end tweezers. The gauze would keep the opening at the skin from sealing up; an abscess has to heal from the inside out or it will recur, and the packed-in gauze holds the cavity open. No one looked at the intern. The senior resident was explaining things to the grandmother, telling her what had been done. The smell lingered in the air, though now much diminished, with the stained gauze pads and other detritus in a red plastic bag in the rolling steel bucket at the edge of the stretcher. The junior resident was cleaning up.

The senior resident said, "This doctor will give you a prescription for antibiotics"—he gestured toward the intern—"and you should return to see us in the clinic in four days so we can take a look to see how Michael is doing. If he is doing okay, this doctor will take out the packing gauze then. Here's the number to call if there are any problems, all right?" The grandmother nodded. The intern went out to get a prescription pad and stamp it with Michael's hospital card from the front desk; he wrote out the right prescription and walked back to the treatment room. By now, Michael was sitting up on the stretcher and his grandmother was helping him put his T-shirt back on. The junior resident had cleaned away all the evidence of what had just happened. The intern handed the grandmother the prescription. "One pill four times a day until you see us, okay? Angie at the front desk will tell you what time to come on Monday." She put the prescription in her purse and led Michael out into the waiting room.

Monday came and the intern had forgotten about abscesses, pus, and vomiting. Sick children and their parents flowed through his days in a steady stream. And then the call from the ER came through on the voice beeper, "Your patient is in the ER treatment room waiting for you." *My patient*, the intern thought, *who do they mean?* He walked down into the treatment room and saw Michael seated on the stretcher, T-shirt on, with a blank, impassive face. His grandmother sat in the chair next to the stretcher.

The intern told Michael to take off his shirt and lie down and then put on plastic gloves and slowly pulled up the edges of the square bandage over the wound. The white tape stuck to Michael's skin, leaving the rough outline of the adhesive on the boy's chest. Under the broad cover of the tape, the mound of five or six square gauze pads stayed on top of the wound, and as the intern peeled them off, the pads gradually became darker with the stain of dried blood and pus. The last pad was still moist with the drainage from the wound. The area around the wound was much less swollen, the skin soft under the touch of the intern's gloved fingers.

As he pressed all around the wound, the intern asked, "Does it hurt here?" and Michael answered with, "Nope."

As the last gauze square came off, the incision wound itself was there, a sharp-edged X on the skin, with the tag of the packing sticking out, a bright white end with a leading edge of darker yellow and brown. There was only a hint of the previous smell.

"Okay," the intern said, "everything looks good. I am going to remove the packing. Just hold still and it'll be over in a minute." But as he moved his hand toward the end of the tape, Michael slapped it away and shouted, "No! Don't touch it!" His voice was as sharp as the slap.

The intern said, "Now hold on, this won't be so bad."

And again, "No!"

The intern held his gloved hands together in front of his chest. Michael raised his head up off the stretcher and tried to turn his body so he could climb down.

"Michael, stop, we have to take the packing out. It will only hurt a bit, but it has to come out. It will feel better when it is out."

"No, don't touch it! I don't want you to touch it! Leave it alone!

"Just stay still. It won't take a minute; you won't even feel it. "

That was a lie. Michael would feel it, but it would not be much more painful than removing the bandages had been. *This is fear of pain, not real pain*, the intern thought. *What is this kid's problem?*

He could feel the sweat building up on the back of his neck near the hairline. He had other things to do. He needed to get this over with.

The grandmother said, "Boy! Let the doctor do his work."

"No!"

There were no tears on Michael's face to plead with her. Just hot defiance.

"Be good, now! Behave!"

"No!"

"Don't embarrass me, boy, be still!"

"No!"

The intern tried again to touch the end of the packing. Michael turned his whole body over, almost facedown.

"No, Michael!" the intern said. "You shouldn't touch the wound. Don't get it dirty. Just turn over, and let me get this." The intern tried to push Michael's shoulder down to keep him from turning.

"I don't want it! Stop it! It's going to hurt!" Michael said with more force but with a bit of a whine at the end of the sentence.

The intern's cheeks were now red and sweat was about to fall through his sideburns onto his face. "Oh, come on, Michael. Be a man. Just let me do this."

Michael rolled over onto his back again and looked the intern in the eye. *Be a man* was the last straw, coming from the intern.

But the intern went for broke. "Okay, here we go." Again Michael's hand flew up to swat the intern away with a slap.

"Just put your hand under your butt, Michael, and hold it; stop making a big deal."

As the intern's hand moved toward his chest for the fourth time, Michael pushed the intern's chest, pushing him off balance. The intern had had enough. "NO! Hold still, *damn it!*" He raised his voice through gritted teeth. "Damn it, just hold still. I am tired of this." And he shoved the boy back onto the stretcher.

The room seemed empty of air. The intern's shirt collar stuck to his neck with sweat. He wanted to get this over with. He had things to do. He didn't want to waste time. *Why can't this kid just grit his teeth? Why can't he stop being such a baby? I am going to get that damned packing out of his chest no matter what. His stupid grandmother is no help. Why is this kid wasting all my time? I have other people waiting for me. I have meetings to go to. I haven't had any breakfast or lunch. Stupid kid, stop being such a baby.*

"Michael! We have to do this. I am going to do this. Now hold still. You can make noise, but don't move. It won't take a moment and then it will be over."

"NO!"

"God damn it, Michael! What is wrong with you?" The intern fixed Michael in his gaze, red-faced, sweating, truly angry. But he was defeated. In a low and threatening voice, nothing left of the reassuring mesmerist now, just the snake with fangs fully showing, he said, "Okay, stay here and think about what a pain in the ass you are. I will give you a few minutes to cool off and cooperate, but then I will come back, and we *will* get this done."

The intern shoved open the treatment doors and stamped out into the hallway, furious. Halfway down the hallway, he caught himself with the realization: *I hate this boy.*

I hate this boy. This child. This sick child. This patient. I hate him. I want this to hurt.

The intern stepped into an alcove in the hallway, put his head in his hands, and exhaled with a guttural sound; his next breath brought a sob flowing with the force of months, maybe years, of anger, humiliation, and shame.

God damn this kid! God damn him for making me be the monster.

After a few moments in the hallway alcove, the intern pulled himself together enough to think. The only way to make this painless would be to use a needle to inject more lidocaine deep into the wound, and the needle stick would hurt far more than simply removing the packing. He didn't want to approach someone with a needle who kept swatting his hand away. Quick removal of the packing would be less painful than an IV, and it isn't appropriate to give a child IV sedation, with all the risk, for this. Topical anesthetic cream would only numb the surface of the skin. There is no solution other than force.

The intern paged the senior surgical resident. When he answered and listened to the story, he was disgusted with the intern's failure to get the job done, but he arrived in a few minutes with three other surgical residents. They walked back into the room and took charge. The surgical resident told Michael to lie down and Michael obeyed. The surgical residents then swarmed the boy, pinning him to the stretcher. One of the surgical residents pulled out the packing with one smooth motion. It took fifteen seconds. Michael made not one sound and no movement.

The senior resident tossed the damp wad of packing into the red-bagged bin and covered the wound with the four-by-four-inch gauze pad the intern had prepared, smoothing the edges down with thick white tape. He turned to the intern with these questions in his look: *What the hell is wrong with you? Have you let this kid get the best of you? What kind of doctor are you?* But he walked out, saying only, "Looks fine. PO antibiotics one more week, no showers. Call with problems."

Michael already had his shirt back on. He climbed down from the stretcher as the intern repeated the instructions from the resident to his grandmother. The intern walked out the door, moving down the hallway to the next exam room, to his next patient, to the next sick child.

4.

The intern became a resident, and then a fellow, and then an attending doctor. He gathered with the others—the mid-thirties parents of the five-month-old in Bed Space 1, the two primary nurses, the social worker, and the cardiologist—in the small windowless room off the end of the ICU corridor. They were waiting for the surgeon.

The child had been in the intensive care unit for five months, since birth. The family knew the nurses well, and they had met with the cardiologist for a few minutes every other day for the past month. The attending was the newcomer, as he had met the family a few days ago. By now he was working in several roles at the hospital, the specialist in lung disease, the medical ethicist, and the palliative care physician.

The child had already had seven open-chest surgeries, and another, contemplated by the surgeon, was a last attempt to find out why the child was "failing to recover," as the surgeon described to the family.

The pediatrician knew the surgery was another attempt to find out why the child was dying, a kind of living autopsy, though he never would have said so out loud. To the family, another surgery was almost meaningless, because in their hearts they knew their child was already gone. The parents said this to the primary nurse, who spoke to the other nurses about it; together they decided to speak to the cardiologist, who did nothing about it, so they paged the palliative care team, and the pediatrician came to the bedside to speak to the family for an hour or so with the nurses and the social worker. After fewer tears than might be expected, the parents asked the pediatrician to help them tell the surgeon they did not want the next surgery; they wanted this to be over for their dear child, they knew she would not survive, they were afraid not of her death but of her continued life, and they needed to feel that their child might die in peace. So the pediatrician spoke to the surgical fellow, who scheduled a meeting with the surgeon.

The surgeon was late, they always are, but blamelessly so since the minutes of their day held more value than most clinicians; someone is always waiting for them and no one minds the wait. A thin man with short salt-and-cinnamon hair and the body of a runner wrapped in blue scrubs walked in without knocking and sat in the chair held open for him.

The pediatrician began. "Dr. --, thank you for coming. We are having this meeting to talk about Marella. You know everyone here but me. I am the pulmonologist and the palliative care doctor. Mr. and Mrs. Ellis would like to talk with you some more about the surgery."

The surgeon started right in, describing the rationale for the surgery. He told the parents that it was not clear that he would find what was wrong, that the cardiac catheterization showed this and that pressure, that the flow in this vein was good but the lungs were still filling up with fluid. He used a technical language that the parents had five months of expertise in understanding. The father, a burly dark-haired man with a thick gold ring on his left hand, was quiet, looking down at his folded hands resting on the smooth white table. The mother's eyes were red and full as she smoothed the front of her cotton blouse and shifted in her chair.

The surgeon finished speaking. The father put his head in his hands and sighed, and one of the nurses put her hand on his shoulder.

The mother said, "Can Marella stand any more surgery, Dr. --? She's been through so much already. She just isn't getting better. Is this the right thing to do?"

"Well, what, do you want to just give up?"

"No, oh no, but maybe she just can't take it. Maybe she's been through enough. Maybe we should let her go to Heaven."

"Well, if that's what you want, we won't do the surgery. It might not have helped anyway." He pushed his chair back from the table.

The father sighed again.

The mother said, "We just don't know."

"Okay, we won't do the surgery. We can take her off the vent this afternoon."

Tears started to fall through the father's hands onto the laminate table.

"Okay, then, I have to move on here." The surgeon stood up and turned toward the door.

"Dr. --," the pediatrician said, "I know Mr. and Mrs. Ellis appreciate everything you have done for Marella over the past months."

"Yes, yes," he said moving toward the door.

"Oh, yes, for everything you have done for us and for Marella, oh yes, Dr. --, yes, oh, thank you, thank you," Mrs. Ellis said.

But the door was already open and Dr. -- was gone. He refused to be thanked. Time to move on to someone who would agree to be saved.

The nurses filed out, back to their patients, and the social worker left to call other family members to come to the hospital. The cardiologist told the family he would get things ready to remove the ventilator later that afternoon.

The pediatrician was there when the machines were disconnected to offer the family words he thought were better than silence, *you loved her very much* and *she fought so hard to get better* and *you did everything you could* and *she's in Heaven now*, even though he wasn't sure anymore if any of those words were true. Those words were all he had to give, and people expected him to say something, though they wouldn't remember exactly what he said. He hoped they forgot they ever needed him.

After the ventilator was turned off and the child had been swaddled and held, and the parents had cried the tears they had saved up for this day, the nurses took over to prepare the child's body for the last journey to the morgue. The pediatrician didn't stay in the room while all the months of belongings, the pillows and get-well cards and stuffed animals and tape players with children's songs and photos of smiling cousins and shells of heart-shaped balloons, all the things that made the hospital room the family's home for five months, were packed up in carts for the family to take down to their car; they would want to keep all this, he knew, though they wouldn't want to look at it for a long time. Instead he left the ICU without speaking to any of the other doctors and walked slowly down the windowless hallway toward the elevator.

He knew he was responsible for saying out loud what others were thinking: miracle becomes tragedy, cure becomes torture, hope becomes sorrow. After all his training, he had learned his place. His job was to walk the halls of the hospital from room to room, from meeting to meeting, his talons shoved down into his white coat, his scaly tail dragging on the floor behind him.

NURSE CLAPPY GETS HIS

A twelve-year-old girl, her hair pulled into a messy ponytail, waits for anyone other than me to walk by the glass walls of her hospital isolation room. She half sits, half lies on a high mechanical bed with gray, hard-plastic rails; seven days ago, she had a lung transplant. The transplant happened when they always seem to, in the early morning hours, but we count the days from the first sunrise after you leave the operating room, so today is Day Eight. A transplant is a new birthday, and we count off the days in an official manner.

She is awake and watching the quiet nurses and doctors enter and leave the room by the glass doors; she is bound to a machine by the bed by a pale-blue, one-inch hose that connects to a clear plastic mask enclosing her nose and mouth, flattening her thin cheeks. A half-inch-wide, dark-blue cloth strap encircles her head, fastened by Velcro, holds her mask in place. A click and hiss sound sixteen times a minute, and the hose attached to the mask shudders as the air pressure shifts up and down. The mask and hose push a column of air down her mouth to the back of her throat through her vocal cords and down her windpipe, past the stubs of her old lungs and the stubs of the stranger's new ones, down into these borrowed lungs, down wet pink tunnels and through tubes with rings of cartilage like a dryer hose and others like sausage casings, and then on down to the final stop at millions of tiny sacs where only two cells separate the air of the outside world from the blood of her body. These millions of dead-end sacs would like to collapse under their own wet weight, but the pressure in the tube and the mask flows into her mouth, down her throat and into her lungs, holding them open, keeping her alive. Awake or asleep, never alone, she wears the mask every hour of the long days and nights. Out of her earshot, we say she is "riding the mask" while her body gets used to the new lungs, if it can.

On this morning she is attached to the bed by more than the mask and the tube. In the crook of her right arm rests an intravenous line we use to draw blood. A larger line runs in the crease between her right leg and crotch, and after it pierces the skin it runs up her inferior vena cava into her right atrium; this monitors the work of her heart as it pumps blood to the new lungs. A plastic tube pierces the radial artery in her left wrist; the end of tube connects to an expensive carpenter's level, sensing the moment-to-moment changes in her blood pressure and drawing two steady waves across a small green screen above her head. Her left hand is splay-taped open onto a blue plastic board covered in white panty-hose fabric for her comfort. Another line, as thin as angel hair, dives into her left forearm to travel up through larger and larger veins to float in the fast-flowing subclavian vein inside her shoulder and chest. Four antibiotics and one antifungal pump through that line in a steady stream, pushed in by mechanical syringes at the foot of the bed. We have poisoned her immune system to prevent it from attacking the new and foreign lungs. Any old germ might kill her in the state she's in. Her right neck holds a supple line for the white liquid fat and the urine-yellow protein solutions that give her body calories because we won't let her eat while she is riding the mask.

Betadine and dried blood have colored her chest yellow-brown, but she was already brownish yellow everywhere, with a shade of green in the daylight, because her liver wasn't well to begin with and a lung transplant hasn't helped. Thumb-thick plastic tubes run through her skin in a row under her armpits and between her ribs, coming to rest between the chest wall and the new lungs, draining out any fluid that accumulates. The tubes dangle down the bed and attach to white-and-blue plastic boxes taped upright to the floor. The girl is awake and alert for the moment. Two days ago we pulled out the tube that went through her mouth past her tongue and into her throat, pushing aside her vocal cords. For five days after the operation, a ventilator pressed machined breaths into her new lungs, too hard and too fast for an awake human to tolerate. But she got a little better and we took that tube out. With that tube out, we can decrease the sedation. With that tube out, she can speak.

The first word she says is "water." Her thirst is desperate, her lips cracked sandpaper, her tongue a flopping cactus. We knew it would be, and we had warned her before the surgery. For days we had been draining every milliliter of fluid out of her with tubes and diuretics. But now she starts pleading, sobbing without tears for a drink, and we will not even give her ice chips. We are withholding water from her and she knows it is deliberate and she wants water now; she cannot be distracted and she keeps asking until it is clear we will not give in. She hates us with the solid hate of a seventh grader. She pouts but doesn't say she hates me. Her throat is sore and dry and she doesn't want to waste her words on me, but I can imagine what she would say.

I take it for a good sign. *She's in there,* I say. *Her head is okay,* I say. *It wasn't damaged by being on the heart-lung pump for the hours of surgery.* I am happy to live with pissed-off silence. I can stand to be thought of as that mean doctor. I know how to wear my practiced smile, the one that says I know what's good for you.

She can't have water. Her swollen body hides liters of fluid, and over the next week it will slowly drain back into her veins. Her body is already full of water; any more will leak straight to her new lungs, and lungs are nothing but living sponges. Fill them up, when they are already touchy, when they are already trying to collapse under their own weight, and she will be in trouble. An hour after water, she will be back on the ventilator, and it will take days to get her back off.

We will not give her water.

So on that morning, she is not in what some more saintly doctor would call a pleasant mood. The nurse and I are standing in the little alcove to the left of the bed, each reading our charts, checking what the consultants have written, entering lab values on various forms, doing the small but constant jobs to keep her body working. The glass doors to the isolation room are closed, but the lights are on. Not much is happening in the room—until a clown shuffles by the door.

The clown is a tall man with granny glasses, a red circle on each cheek, a pair of yellow-plaid carnival barker pants, two floppy shoes, a long white coat, and a nurse's cap. He is a professional hospital clown. His name tag says Nurse Clappy. He is the Head Clown in the Clown Care Unit, a trio of roving clowns who wander the hallways of the hospital dressed as doctors and nurses, paid for, or so it is said, by a family whose child died years ago, though they could just as easily have set up a fund for social workers. As he passes by the closed glass isolation door, he looks inside. He smiles at the girl on the high bed. He raises his eyebrows and his nursing cap shifts backward on his balding head.

His cap is absurd and he knows it. No nurse has worn a cap at a Boston teaching hospital since 1975. No doctor under fifty and certainly no child alive today has ever seen a nurse in her cap outside of a TV rerun. And of course male nurses never wore caps. So Nurse Clappy is in drag; he is wandering the halls of a children's hospital in nurse-cap drag, strumming his ukulele to brighten the day of all those he encounters. And now he is here, outside the isolation room, peering through the glass and smiling his painted-on smile.

He has caught her eye. She looks at him through the glass, and her returned look is all the clown needs. Nurse Clappy now opens his mouth even wider and smiles so you can see his back teeth. His eyes crinkle as he faces the glass door, preparing his act. She is still looking at him, eyes clear and focused from her raised bed, turning her head to the left to look at him head on. Suddenly he throws his arms open wide, in a howdy-doodle-do, and mimes *Well, hello there!* He waves with his right hand and then pulls a full-akimbo back arch with a half-rightward head tilt. She is still looking right at him. Her right hand begins to move up and off the bed.

He's got her now, he thinks. He will whisk her away from her bed of pain to his Big Top, to the smell of sawdust and lion sweat, to the *ooh* and the *aahh* of watching the daring net-less fliers, to the plumed beauty standing on white horseback. He will be her guide; she will take his padded white glove in hand and escape this room, if only for a minute.

He cocks his head to the left and lifts the lapel of his long white coat to smell his plastic flower. She is looking right at him. Her right hand is still moving, slowly, side to side for a moment and then back up, bent at the elbow and palm down, unsteady but determined. He squirts himself with his flower. He gasps in surprise and pulls out a handkerchief of many colors to dry his tiny glasses. She is still looking right at him and her hand is still rising slowly off the bed, palm down with fingers slightly parted, slowly rotating out from her body, little finger tucking under and thumb rising.

Is she going to wave? She is going to wave! Nurse Clappy loves to play the waving game, to send those happy smoke signals through the glass walls, to share a greeting between fun buddies across seven feet of open room.

Her hand is sideways now, thumb on top, and her eyes are bright. She has lifted her head off the bed a bit to make sure she can see him over the top of the mask. He is smiling and waving and she is waiting and watching, making sure he is watching her.

Her index finger twitches slightly. No, he sees, it's deliberate; she is going to wave! She loves his clown song, his happy serenade! She turns her hand over even more, and her fingers curl, but not all of them. The middle finger stays upright. The middle finger, the one with the white plastic clamp that measures oxygen in the blood, does not curl. It stays outstretched as she gathers the others into a fist.

She is waving, all right. And Nurse Clappy catches her special wave.

A low throaty growl fills the room. A panting raspy sound flows off her high bed. Short, sharp intakes of air and low rumbling laughter rise into the air. Her mouth corners into a smile through the plastic mask. Her tight and tired face comes alive with laughter.

Our mouths are open, the nurse's and mine. We don't even try not to laugh. We just laugh and smile and wheeze and laugh and she joins us, laughing and laughing. We don't say anything; we just stand at the side of her bed and laugh, looking back and forth at each other and at her, all three of us stopping and then starting again when we look at each other, and then we try to be serious but we laugh again and giggle and snort and cough and wheeze and sigh and laugh and laugh and laugh until we have washed the room clean with our laughter, filled it enough to rinse out the stale smells of blood and Betadine and fear and anger and worry, if only for this minute. We three laugh until we have laughed enough for ourselves and for each other, for the last week and the week to come. And then we go back to work.

Four days later, she sleeps too soundly. She lets the nurse change her drains without a protest. Her eyes are open, but she looks through me, not angry, not asleep, not awake. I call the surgeon, and he calls the radiologist. We connect her to the portable IV pumps as fast as we can and head to the reserve elevator down the head CT suite. We hover over the technician's monitor, watching the cuts come into view. We see it right away, a circle of white on the left, and it gets bigger as the machine moves down her head. A ball of fungus has settled down comfortably inside her brain; a ball of fungus snuck through the hole we made in her immune defenses.

We move more slowly going back upstairs. I make some calls to

Infectious Disease, to Neurology, to her family. The surgeon shows the CT to her family and I have nothing to add. We do everything we can over the next thirty-six hours, everything we can think to do, but we know, all of us, that all we can do will not be enough. She dies on Day 12.

Fourteen years later, I remember only parts of this. I do not remember the nurse's name. I do not remember the color of the girl's hair or if she had sisters or brothers or anything about her family. I do not remember if all my memories are right; maybe I mixed up two little girls, maybe it was the other surgeon who was there, maybe it was morning not evening, maybe it was Day 7 or Bed Space 10. I don't trust my memory for that sort of detail. My grief for her flows into my grief for all the children who died. But I do remember the beautiful sound of her rasping laughter. I remember the smile on her face and in her eyes. Every time I see an oxygen sensor I remember her raised finger of protest against indignity, how she wiped the painted smile off the face of that clown. Some days I go to work sustained by the hope that today, somewhere in the country, some clown will get flipped a defiant bird by a thirsty girl with new lungs in a glass-walled room, and that someone will be there to laugh with her.

COGNITIVE SPARING

When Luke was born his mother knew something was wrong. She never heard that first cry of a newborn, the high raspy wail we all connect with the shock of loud and bright life. She never saw him raised above the blue surgical drapes covering her from the waist down, never saw him up in the air in the obstetrician's arms, never felt his warm body on her chest or his small hand gripping her finger in greeting.

Instead, all the yelling and the pushing and the encouragement in the delivery room was followed by a sudden and heavy quiet. She felt her husband's hand tighten in hers. She heard the low whisper of a nurse on the phone, "Get the peds guys, *right now*." The door exploded with doctors in scrub shirts. No one looked at her when they entered, but then she began to have more contractions, and the obstetrician looked her in the eyes and said, "One more slow push and the placenta will be out." His gloved hand massaged her abdomen but she didn't feel it. She was listening to the tense voices of the doctors. She could see them crowded around a high table to her right, but she couldn't see what they were doing. Was Luke still in the delivery room? She could only hear low voices and the click and ping of monitors. She craned her neck to glimpse a small gray foot through the wall made by the backs of the doctors and nurses. She turned to look into her husband's face and saw his fear for the first time.

Away from her sight, the doctors placed a flexible clear tube down Luke's limp throat and began to inflate his lungs by squeezing a floppy black bag attached to a pressure dial. They put silver leads the size of nickels with thin red and black wires on Luke's chest, and the monitor on the side of the table showed only a flat, green horizontal line. With his thumb curled under the first and second fingers of his gloved right hand, one of the doctors began to make rapid hard tapping motions on Luke's chest as one nurse pumped air into Luke's lungs and the other nurse drew up medications from the code cart.

Three long minutes later, in an ante-room next to the delivery suite, Luke's heart began to beat on its own. The tube in Luke's throat was now attached by a larger tube to a ventilator, a blue box the size of a toaster that pulsed and shook at the side of his basinet. An IV ran into the crook of his left arm.

Fifteen minutes after that, still in that small room, his body began to shake, his arms and legs flailing open as if to hug the air above the bed. This startled quivering was seizure activity, six of them less than an hour after his birth. A newborn seizing resembles a wet puppy shaking off a chill—there is trembling and flailing and shivering that would cause the untrained to rush for a blanket, wrap the baby up, do anything to keep them warm. But to the doctors who witnessed it, a neonatology fellow and the two pediatric residents, this seizure was bad news: something was seriously wrong with this baby's brain.

And so, forty-five minutes later, after she had been wheeled into the recovery room by nurses with too-hard smiles and quiet eyes, Luke's mother met a new doctor in a long white coat and a green scrub hat. He was the neonatologist, and he told her he'd come to the recovery room to introduce himself, and to say that things for Luke did not look good.

Ten days later, after an EEG, an MRI, and seven different examinations by the pediatric neurologists, Luke was diagnosed with a catastrophic injury to his brain. His parents were stunned. The pregnancy had gone to term, and there had been no hint of a problem. His mother had not been sick. This was their first child, but they had nieces and nephews who were all healthy, and they both came from large families. No one in the family could remember any child being seriously sick. The doctors could not give a precise cause of the problem, whether something had happened in the last few months of the pregnancy or whether something had been wrong all along—this sort of damage can go unseen by an ultrasound or any prenatal testing.

The parents talked several times each day with the doctors and nurses to review the various tests done on Luke. His heart had a normal structure and was beating without any difficulty after the initial trouble in the delivery room. His kidneys and liver were working normally. Everything but his brain seemed to be perfect. His parents reviewed the brain scans with the doctors and with the neurology consultants; they were told it was very unlikely that Luke would ever walk or speak. The scans showed either severe scarring or absence of the brain areas responsible for movement, speech, sight, and hearing: the prognosis was that Luke would never sit; never crawl or walk; never see, hear, or speak. The brain tissue had atrophied, meaning that it had either never fully developed or that it had been deprived of oxygen or blood at some time before his birth. There was nothing unusual about the pregnancy or the delivery because Luke's body was being regulated by his mother's body—as long as mother and child were in sync, Luke could survive, but on its own, his body could not function. Being born would have killed him had the doctors not intervened to restart his heart, breathe for him, and stop the seizures with drugs. The ventilator was now keeping Luke alive by pushing air into his lungs, inflating them like twin balloons, and then pausing to let them deflate on their own from the recoil of the spongy tissue and the rib cage. The lungs were normal, but they needed the electronic brain of the ventilator to tell them to breathe.

Twelve days after their baby's birth, and after discussion with the doctors and nurses, Luke's parents asked that the ventilator be removed from their son and he be allowed to die without "unnatural" delay. When the clinical team expressed some reservations over this, Luke's parents asked for the Hospital Ethics Committee to consult with them. One of the nurses in the neonatal ICU had told them about the committee, a group of hospital employees led by nurses and doctors with specialized training in ethics who could be called to the bedside to help parents and clinicians make difficult decisions, usually in matters of life and death. The committee at this hospital was unusual, as it also included parents of children who had been seriously ill at the hospital. When a consultation was requested, a three-person team was assembled; in the most difficult cases, a parent was always a member of the consultation team. These three people would meet with the clinicians and the family—sometimes separately, sometimes together—to explore the various options. The committee members might make recommendations, but they did not make any final decisions. In most cases they had a mediating role, helping families and physicians discuss heartbreaking topics and reasonable conclusions about the next steps. In a case like Luke's, the ethics consult team would meet with the family and the doctors, listen to everyone involved, and meet again with everyone in the same room to provide an opportunity for the clinicians and the family to agree on a plan.

For the ethics consult team, the question of removing a ventilator was not a new one. In the past decade there had been a consensus in American medicine and medical ethics that a treatment could be refused by a patient, or by the parents of a child, if the burdens of the treatment outweighed the current and potential benefits of the treatment. There was also a consensus that being on a ventilator without the expectation of recovery, attached permanently to a machine, was a significant burden for a child.

But the issue was not exactly whether it was acceptable to disconnect the ventilator, although that is the way it is seen by those outside the medical world. The ventilator was routinely disconnected from the tube in Luke's throat every day in order to move him or to suction out the tube, and the tube itself was changed every so often. When this had been done, Luke did not breathe on his own, and a resuscitation bag had to be used during these routines. From this, and from the damage seen on the brain scans, the doctors did not expect that Luke would begin to breathe on his own without the machine. What Luke's parents wanted was for the doctors to agree not to replace the tube and the ventilator if it was clear that Luke could not survive without it.

In short: Would the doctors allow him to die when they could keep him alive?

After discussion with Luke's parents, the clinical team and the ethics committee agreed that "refusal" of the ventilator was reasonable. This decision was not surprising: it was the norm to agree if parents wanted to disconnect a child from a ventilator if the child had no prospect of getting off the ventilator and if there was also severe brain damage, so that the prospect for recovery was near zero.

The vocabulary in these instances is very specific. Parents usually say, "the child will die after the ventilator is removed," whereas pediatricians and ethicists almost uniformly say, "the child will be allowed to die after the ventilator is removed." The different locutions are telling. "Allowed" implies that the pediatricians still have the power to save the child, though they have declined to use it, whereas the parents see the death as simply happening because of the child's illness.

The difference in vocabulary captures decades of struggle to form a consensus about advanced technology in pediatric ethics. As in adult medicine, the development of life-sustaining technology occurred before the implications of the technology could be fully considered. For severely ill children, especially infants, the often unstated assumption is that every attempt should be made to save the child's life. Much of the new technology for infants was first used in premature infants and was intended to be a placeholder to support the child while healing or maturation took place; the assumption was that either that the child would survive to live without the technology or die no matter what technology was employed. It was not expected that children might linger as neither success nor failure, but if they did, it was assumed that the scarcity of any advanced technology would mean that no infants would be chronically dependent on the technology for their survival.

As it turned out, there was no scarcity. The system of health care, both the science and the funding, evolved so that life could be sustained in almost every case. Newer equipment, smaller ventilators, more experience with the management of permanent tracheostomy tubes, and increasingly specialized skill at managing the needs of these infants led to the ability to keep children on ventilators for decades, creating an entire new population of children who were permanently dependent on technology to survive. This possibility would have stunned those who first implemented the technology, since they had considered these machines to be a bridge toward health, not a destination. That a child might live permanently dependent on technology like a ventilator was, at the beginning, thought to be a terrible outcome. As is often the case, we physicians focused more on the consequences of failure than those of success. Once our skill at the use of technology had advanced to make its use routine and widespread, a population of children dependent on machines emerged. Questions about the appropriateness of creating children permanently dependent on technology quickly developed, with some arguing that this was a perversion of our duty to children and others believing that saving the child's life should always be the presumption.

Faced with an apparently irreducible conflict about the right way to use technology in young children, modern medical ethics abandoned the effort to find the best substantive policy and focused instead on a debate about who had the authority to decide in a particular instance. Someone would have to make decisions about when to use life-sustaining technology in a specific child—but who should make this decision? The physicians? The parents? The courts? Slowly, an American consensus took shape: Parents could decide to remove a treatment, even if the treatment was sustaining the child's life, only if the burden of the treatment outweighed the benefit. Exactly what constituted a burden or a benefit was a matter of interpretation in individual cases. Physicians had to agree that the benefits were few and the burdens were high before turning the decision over to the parents to continue or refuse as they saw best for the child.

If the parents agreed that the intervention was more burdensome than beneficial for their child, the physicians could allow the child to die. In addition, the consensus held that allowing the child to die could take two morally equivalent courses. First, the doctors could decide not to begin a therapy considered more burdensome than beneficial. This is called *withholding*. But this approach is rarely taken, as doctors and parents usually wanted to try new therapies because of the possibility of efficacy, especially in very young children with the potential for growth and development. Even if the odds are slim, doctors want to take action against tragedy. We are optimists, or at least pediatricians usually are, and we want to try to rescue a child. So discussions over invasive therapies usually took the second route of stopping a therapy if it becomes more burdensome than beneficial. This is called *withdrawing*. In the world of medical ethics, withholding and withdrawing are equivalent.

Given the option, Luke's parents decided to withdraw the ventilator. Luke's bassinet was wheeled over to a side room in the ICU to give his parents some privacy in the expectation of his death. Luke's primary nurse put him in his mother's lap in a pale-blue blanket and white cotton onesie and gently removed the ventilator tube from Luke's mouth, wiping his lips with a cool cloth. Luke's mother hugged him through her tears.

Luke took some breaths, his mouth open with his lips tented upward, pulling and tugging with the muscles in his neck and chest; he did not open his eyes or cry. He was floppy and still in his mother's arms; he made a soft wet noise with each breath in, and his lips quivered with an exhale. His mother watched him through tears, saying, *We love you, sweet baby, Mommy and Daddy love you, go to Heaven, it's okay, sweet baby. We love you, we love you.* Luke took a short, sharp breath in, a hiccough or a gasp, without struggle. He was still, and then another hiccough breath. And another. The onlookers thought each breath might be the last one, but each breath was followed by another, coming quicker and quicker, and then steadily he began to breathe through his nose, as an infant should. He settled into a regular rhythm of inhale and exhale, but he did not open his eyes or move his arms. He did not cough or gasp, but he kept breathing shallow, steady breaths, in and out, in and out. The oxygen saturation monitor, via a red light taped with a crêpe-like beige bandage to his small palm, showed a value good enough for an infant.

Luke was breathing on his own. And he kept doing it, without the need for extra oxygen, without the need for the ventilator, even when he seemed to be asleep—though since he did not move and never cried, the difference between awake and asleep was slight.

Everyone was surprised. Everyone was relieved to be wrong. Later, blood tests showed he could maintain a normal amount of oxygen and carbon dioxide in his blood. Luke did not need the ventilator.

A few days later, after Luke had had a chance to adjust to breathing on his own, his mother and the nurses tried to feed him with a bottle. Prior to this time, he had been fed like all babies on a ventilator: by means of a thin tube passed through his nose, down the esophagus, and into his stomach. An intubated baby cannot be fed by mouth, because the tube for the ventilator is in the way in his mouth, and because the suck-swallow-breathe rhythm of infant feeding is disrupted by the work of the ventilator. Luke was fed by tube for a few days after the ventilator was removed, and then the transition to a bottle started. Most infants do not have to be taught how to suck from a bottle, but those who have been sick need time to adjust. The reflexes that whoever designs babies put in place are strong: when a nipple is near the side of an infant's mouth, they will turn toward it; when anything nipple-shaped is put in their mouth, they will try to suck on it.

But Luke didn't do any of these things. He did nothing. He didn't suck or gag or cry. He didn't react. He didn't cry near feeding time, even if feeding time was late. The longer the nurses tried, even those nurses most skilled at feeding the most difficult-to-feed infants, using every nipple shape, every size nipple opening, every position and strategy, whether formula or breast milk, the worse it got. He had no gag reflex, so any formula dripped into his mouth would pool at the back of his throat and go partly down into his lungs, making him at risk for pneumonia. Luke appeared distressed by the attempts to feed him. He acted as if he were being hurt by any contact. He seemed to get no consolation from being held or cuddled. He had two states of being: a blank and quiet state of what appeared to be complete nonawareness, and an agitated state of what looked like discomfort. Leaving him alone, wrapped in a blanket in the basinet, could return him to the blank state; any interaction seemed to cause distress.

At the end of the third week of Luke's life, it became clear that Luke could never feed from a bottle. The clinical team now wanted to place a more permanent feeding tube through Luke's abdomen into his stomach. This is the usual practice when an infant cannot feed by mouth for whatever reason, because the tube through the nose into the stomach becomes displaced very easily and requires frequent removal and repositioning; it also increases the risk of food going into the lung in an infant without a gag reflex. It isn't a long-term solution.

His parents objected, saying that the feeding tube was just another artificial way of keeping Luke alive. Wasn't the feeding tube just like the ventilator, they asked, a way of prolonging Luke's death?

But this time the clinical team was reluctant to agree. They believed that the burden of a permanent feeding tube was much less than that of the ventilator. After all, many children in the hospital needed assistance with feeding tubes, and unlike a ventilator, a child with a feeding tube could easily go home, grow up, attend school, and so on. We pediatricians, particularly those accustomed to treating severely ill children, did not view having a feeding tube as burdensome enough to justify withholding it.

More importantly, the clinicians believed that allowing Luke to die by not feeding him was cruel and unnatural. Feeding a baby was an ethical command, and withholding food was nothing like withholding a ventilator. Deciding not to feed a baby bordered on heresy. All babies would die if we didn't feed them, even healthy babies, so it seemed particularly perverse not to feed a baby by any means available.

The clinicians also believed that Luke had an unusual brain injury; the consultants used the phrase *cognitive sparing* to describe a likely future life that included blindness, deafness, and an inability to walk or talk, with one important difference: Luke would have only moderate cognitive limitations. The areas of his brain in charge of cognitive thought were spared from the damage to the other areas of the brain, at least on the CT scans. Wouldn't not feeding him be starving him to death and justifying it because of his physical handicaps?

That anyone would allow any child to "starve to death" was a volatile idea in a pediatric community. But an even more important aspect of the minefield of allowing a child to die without feeding was the history of pediatrician nontreatment of children with Down syndrome. Up until the late 1970s, it was relatively common that children with Down syndrome would not be operated on to relieve a straightforward intestinal obstruction or cardiac defect, something we would automatically repair for any other infant; the infant with Down or several other syndromes would be "allowed to die" because of the pediatricians' and parents' judgment that a life with the cognitive and social deficits of Down syndrome was an unbearable burden. This view was widely accepted in society and in medical circles, but by the time Luke was born, the consensus was that this approach was not just wrong but misguided and openly hostile to those with disabilities. Subsequent studies demonstrated that physicians, perhaps because of their own life experience, overvalued the importance of cognitive skills when assessing quality of life compared to parents and the public. Further studies suggested that parents held the same views and often similarly undervalued the quality of life for children with intellectual disabilities.

So, as the consensus was developing that individuals could refuse burdensome treatments even if they were life-sustaining, a similarly powerful consensus was developing that children were appropriate candidates for high-tech medical interventions in spite of a perceived low quality of life. Luke was caught between these two views in medical ethics: on the one hand, adults and parents of children have been given the power to control their medical care even if doing so leads to an earlier death; on the other hand, the decisions of parents and physicians to forgo medical intervention because of the poor quality of life of a child were increasingly suspect.

In a subsequent letter to the attending physicians, nurses, and ethics committee members, Luke's parents began with these lines: "We are asking for your help in arranging palliative care for Luke and advising us regarding options for keeping him comfortable so

that he may pass away peacefully and without unnatural delays. . . .
We have searched our hearts and minds from every angle we could
find, and we've constantly prayed for God to guide us in making a
decision in Luke's best interest. We have asked questions and listened carefully to all of you for three weeks. We have involved the
ethics people and we have listened to opinions and comments from
everyone involved."

The letter closes with this paragraph: "We are Luke's parents—
Mommy and Daddy. No person on earth loves or wants him so much
as we do. But we are willing to let him go to God. And so, we ask
you to support us and help us make Luke's passing as comfortable,
peaceful, and natural as possible. If and when all artificial measures
are removed, we all will truly have turned the decision over to God."

The ethics consultation team also assessed Luke's situation in
a report to the parents and the full ethics committee. While the
committee agreed that Luke's parents had his best interest in mind,
they were concerned that just as the prognosis of being unable to
breathe on his own turned out to be wrong, there might be uncertainty in his neurological prognosis. Though it was clear he would
be severely disabled, and would never see or hear, perhaps he could
develop what the committee called "relational ability," a connection
to others in the world that would give Luke's life meaning regardless
of his limitations.

The ethics consultation team asked the full ethics committee to help
deliberate about the parents' request, and this is when I first heard
Luke's story. I was one of the four hospital ethicists; I had not been
on call when the original discussion about removing the ventilator
had taken place. But when the question became whether it was per-
missible not to place the feeding tube, more of the ethics committee
members, and particularly the ethicists, got involved.

The challenge for the clinicians and the parents and the ethicists were to fit Luke's unique clinical status to these somewhat opposing poles of ethical consensus. The clinical facts were unique to Luke, of course. In contrast to almost every other baby, Luke seemed to get no pleasure out of eating and had no distress from hunger. He was not soothed by a full belly and not troubled by an empty one. Luke seemed to have almost no reaction at all to feeding, a sort of indifference that indicated just how damaged his neurologic circuitry was. It is the extremely rare baby who is not soothed by food, no matter his or her condition, and it was hard to believe that not being fed wasn't a kind of suffering, but those who observed him most closely, even ardent supporters of placing the feeding tube, had to agree that there were no observable signs of distress from hunger or comfort from food in Luke.

The more difficult issue was the severity of Luke's brain injury. His neurologic deficit was substantially more severe than any child with Down syndrome; in fact, the very thing that makes children with Down syndrome so socially engaging, their openness and friendliness and capacity for relationships, would be beyond Luke's reach, as he would be immobile, blind, deaf, and speechless. Even in a situation where assessment of quality of life in the future is difficult with an infant, there was no question that Luke's life would be far more limited than even the most severely affected child with Down syndrome.

The question of Luke's potential for "relational ability" was a nearly impossible one to assess. In an important sense, this would depend on persons other than Luke. Although Luke might not be very responsive, those who cared for him might come to love him deeply and perhaps read in his involuntary signs more of a connection than was biologically plausible. Many of us knew well of cases of parents of severely disabled children who wrapped their lives around the child, emotionally, spiritually, and organizationally, such that the child played the central role in the lives of the parent and the family. These children were cared for scrupulously and were included in almost every family event, even though there was no evidence to an impartial observer that the child was aware of his surroundings at all. This is the great unknowable of parenting, that love for a child can transform reality into a comfortable and loving fantasy. The fantasy was uncomfortable for some clinicians, many of whom avoided these families out of discomfort with what they saw as a pathological aspect to the parent-child bond. On the other hand, who were we to decide the meaning of love that a parent has for a child?

But what if the people around Luke did not come to see him in this way? What if the ability to be comforted by feeding played an important role in an infant soliciting from others the type of projected affection that signifies a relationship? Would Luke then become what we all dreaded, a being in a bed cared for with skill but indifference in an institutional setting? And could we as physicians make the decision that Luke should live only if we could be certain that he would be unconditionally loved all his life—an improbably high standard—or that a life with indifferent relationships with others is a life not worth living?

No one on the ethics committee and none of the clinicians could be certain that placing or not placing the feeding tube was in Luke's best interest. They were concerned that just as the prognosis of being unable to breathe on his own turned out to be wrong, Luke might recover some unexpected neurological function and his brain might adapt to the damage in some way as yet poorly understood. They could not balance their imperfect knowledge of his physiological and behavioral future against their concern about prolonging his suffering. The clinicians and some members of the ethics team saw Luke as an "exceptional" child, and in conversation with Luke's parents they used the analogies of Christopher Reeve and Helen Keller to talk of the possible futures for Luke. They believed that

Luke's brain injury was unlike many other infants with severe brain injuries. They believed that his life, while difficult, could be worth living. They were uncertain in this prognosis, and they favored waiting and performing more examinations and possibly more brain scans. They felt that if they turned out to be wrong, a feeding tube could always be withdrawn later, so there was no disadvantage in waiting for more information.

Luke's parents saw things quite differently. They saw his continued life as a tragedy. Luke's parents interpreted his situation as a kind of living hell, trapped inside a body that could never work and tormented, perhaps, by an awareness of what he was missing. They were not consoled by the idea that his cognitive ability might not be impaired, because any awareness he might have developed was, in their eyes, just more evidence of the potential horror of his continued life. Better that Luke should die unaware of his situation than live so disconnected from those who loved him *and* be aware of his disconnection. They viewed the feeding tube as an artificial intrusion into what otherwise would have been the peaceful death of a child whose life was not meant to be. They feared not Luke's death, but his continued life.

At stake here were two different narratives of a life. The parents told a story of a tragic accident of fate, a life not meant to be, a life in God's hands. The doctors told a story of triumph over disability, of possible rescue from fate, of uncertainty requiring more testing and observation.

How do we imagine the story of a child like Luke? We can invoke stories about innocent suffering, the injustice of the world, the need for heroic rescue, or the pain of tragedy.

It is no coincidence that we pediatricians often see ourselves as warriors against illness and despair. The need to be seen as heroic may be necessary to permit us to harm children in the pursuit of healing them. While an adult may make sense of the suffering required to cure a serious illness, a child cannot, and adopting the role of heroic rescuer shields us both from the child's indignation and from our own sense that we are hurting the ones we intend to protect. Pediatricians may need this strong heroic role to allow us to inflict suffering on protesting children, to permit us to make them sicker now so that they may be well later. Yet the rescue role constrains the pediatrician by making it difficult to treat a child when a cure—the rescue—is not possible.

Families also invoke stories as a way of describing themselves and their goals. Family stories have characters (in many senses of the word), some living, some dead; families have stories that persist over generations; families have internal tales that explicitly or implicitly frame the meaning of the present with the events of the past and the future. Family narratives shape what counts as a good parent, a good child, and a good life. Luke's parents see Heaven as real. They see God's hand where the pediatricians see bad luck. His parents see their role as protectors not simply of Luke's existence, but of the imaginative nature of his future life. They cannot accept keeping him alive to forestall their grief at his death.

Luke's family and the clinicians were at an impasse, and days of discussion did not change the position of either side. Nor could the members of the ethics consultation team come to an agreement. The clinicians offered to transfer Luke to another advanced-care hospital if the parents wanted to do so, but the parents trusted the doctors and nurses they already knew, and depended on them. They could not move to a new place with strangers; better to stay among friends who disagreed. Luke's parents knew the doctors were trying to do the best thing for Luke, just as they were, and both sides hoped that something about Luke might change to make the decision easier. Maybe he would start to take the bottle, if only he were hungrier. Maybe he would not be able to keep breathing. Maybe he would move or cry, or open his eyes. Maybe Luke would send the adults some signal, a sign that they could interpret as his wishes. But he was still and quiet and ignored the bottle and kept breathing, slowly and steadily, for two more weeks.

At five weeks of life, perhaps because of the power of the clinical team, Luke's parents agreed to insert a feeding tube through his stomach wall. Luke tolerated the surgery and returned to the intensive care unit to recover, even though he no longer needed that level of care. Plans were made to discharge him home with tube feedings and some home nursing care for part of the day.

I have come to see Luke's life as an indictment of modern medical ethics as a system for assisting families and clinicians in examining the moral aspects of medical care. We physicians have the power to change and manipulate fate, but we do not have the shared values that would allow us to make difficult decisions under conditions of moral uncertainty. Managing the uncertainty of a practice that involves decisions about the value of life and the meaning of suffering requires something modern medicine lacks: a consensus about the moral meaning of what we do. Are we guardians of choice or champions of the weak? Do we have an understanding of what it means to be a good, or good enough, parent; of what it means to balance the obligations we have to our children against our own needs? Have the precepts we enshrined about the autonomy of the patient allowed us to enjoy a comfortable moral abdication and become highly esteemed technicians with only a limited moral stake in the outcome of our work?

I am clear about it now: we should not have placed the feeding tube.

Once the tube was placed, and under those circumstances, Luke's parents could no longer tell a story about God's mercy or Heaven. We physicians interceded so as to make that story implausible or impossible. What possible way might they see God now? As the source of suffering without meaning? As the judge of His believers who did not believe enough to make the difficult choice? His parents could not tell a story of their devotion to Luke or their faith in the afterlife being strong enough to overcome the inertia of the technocratic medical system. They knew in their hearts what was right and we would not let them do it, so they could not see themselves as the parents who did what was best. We left them a story of a half devotion to their son.

We as doctors and ethicists could not tell a story of our own good judgment and wisdom, of our ability to make a difficult moral call under conditions of uncertainty. We could not say that we had the courage of our convictions because we yielded those convictions under a mask of uncertainty, fooling ourselves about Luke's future so that we would not have to make the hard decision of deciding his fate. We used a common feature of medicine, its fundamental prognostic uncertainty, as a false distraction from our duty to take a deliberate action; the backward slide into placing the feeding tube was a victory of protocol more than ethics. The problem is not that the prognosis was wrong or even that it was uncertain—the problem is that we let uncertainty determine morality.

We might remove the feeding tube now, of course. But this will not happen for the same reasons that the tube was replaced: we will not remove a feeding tube that works and provides no discomfort. There was a moment when we could have let Luke die, but that moment has passed. There was a moment when we could have co-authored the story of Luke's life with his parents in a way that their actions could now be a comfort and a succor, but that moment has passed. There was a moment when we doctors could have affirmed the best story of our profession by embracing uncertainty as a chance to do the right thing; we could have accepted the chance of being wrong in order to act rightly, but that moment has passed, too.

Luke now resides in a pediatric nursing home, in a room with four cribs. He does not move or cry much, and he does not respond to light or sound. He is gaining weight because he is being fed through the tube every six hours. He does not like to be touched. His parents visit every week and every holiday. His crib is festooned with photos of the family celebrations and events he did not attend. There has been no further discussion of removing his feeding tube.

THIS WILL STING AND BURN

The voice on the phone says, "I have your biopsy results."

I never give bad results to my patients over the phone. I am lucky that the type of bad news I give can be readied while the parents and baby wait after an appointment, but sometimes I do have to call to ask a parent to meet me at the hospital: "Sometime today is best, I think." When I deliver bad news in person, I can see the parents' reaction and adapt. I am experienced at telling mothers the test is positive, the baby has a diagnosis with no cure, cystic fibrosis, the terrible disease you read about on the internet after your pediatrician told you the screening test was positive. Except that the disease isn't at all like what you read about—what you read is out of date and these kids can do pretty well these days. If I can see their reactions I know when it is time to say, "You can't believe what you read, just like you can't listen to Aunt Martha or that woman at church," because there is always somebody one who "knew someone with that" and says, "there was that girl in fourth grade, don't you remember her, or was that cerebral palsy, is that the same thing?" I can't know if it's time to make fun of fictional Aunt Martha or that lady from church if we are on the phone. I can't know if my techniques are working if we aren't in the same room. I have thought for years about how mothers and fathers take my bad news. Medical students, residents, and fellows watch me to learn how to deliver a diagnosis, and I use a mixture of kindness and reassuring authority, or so I think.

Since the dermatologist is calling me directly instead of telling me to come in to her office, I assume that the biopsy has come back fine. I didn't intend to have a skin biopsy. A new job, a new house, and new insurance drove me to make the appointment. I had no suspicions; it was just a checkup, a preventive thing you do once you are middle-aged. I took the first morning appointment, because I know how the schedule explodes as the day goes on, and the complaints get less clear, and the diagnoses pile up. We doctors ought to know that reassurance takes longer than expected, but we never seem to schedule for that. I sat in the waiting room alone on a teal plastic chair and read the posters about droopy necks and sagging eyelids, privacy laws and copayments. The room was swimming in country-pop music from overhead speakers.

As I always do, I brought my typed-up page with chief complaint, past medical history, medications, allergies, and so on in the correct format, a signal that I was an insider at a doctor's office. I debated with myself whether to tell the front-office staff I am a doctor; sometimes I want to play the spy and see how they treat the civilians. When it's nothing big, like this checkup, I usually pretend I am a regular person with the receptionist or the clinic assistant, but I always come clean in the exam room. I never joke about being a civilian with the doctor.

The nursing assistant calls me into the office and doesn't take my blood pressure or pulse or weight. She just tells me, "Take off everything but your underpants and get into this gown. The doctor will be right with you."

This doctor, the dermatologist, is a thin woman with thin hair, a pair of small, squared-off tortoise shell glasses riding the ridge of her thin nose and a gray boiled-wool sweater jacket with green accents; I get the idea she is not much of a jokester. Like everyone else alive, I hate hospital gowns, so when she comes in the room I am sitting on the exam table naked except for my boxers and my glasses, and she begins looking me over right away, starting with my face and my bald spot. At first she talks to me while she does her work, but once she moves to my arms and hands, all her chat runs out and we proceed in silence. Between my fingers, over my elbows, under my arms, she is looking; pushing aside my chest hair to the right and the left, letting it fall back into place; bending down to look at my thighs and knees, and on down to my shins, she is looking. She brushes her hands along the tops of both feet and spreads my toes for a look, and I stand up and turn around so she can see my calves, the back of my knees, and then up to my lower back, where she stops and says, "Hunh." She continues up my back and ruffles though the hair at the back of my neck, looking.

And then I feel her fingers slide coolly over my lower back again and she says, "Hmm, how long has this been here?"

I stand up straighter, sucking in my gut, and say, "I can't see it, I don't know what you mean."

She says, "It's just a precaution, but I think we better biopsy that. Can you come back tomorrow afternoon?"

Of course I can. That was what I came to the office for, a checkup and a precaution. So the next day I was facedown on the crinkly white paper on her exam table and she did the biopsy, five stitches, no shower for a few days, keep it covered, we'll call you on Tuesday.

So here she is, calling on Tuesday.

The voice on the phone says, "The biopsy shows malignant melanoma, stage two."

After that sentence, I can't understand what she is saying. Her voice is quick and light but the words bypass my brain, flowing into my left ear and out of my right hand in blue ink onto the lined yellow legal pad I keep by my computer. My handwriting is clear and strong and follows along the lines of the paper, but I feel small and weak and quiet. When she pauses for a breath I write *malignant melanoma* in block letters at the top of the page, and underline it. Then I put the date on the page, like I always do. She talks about the depth of the lesion and the presence of mitotic figures in the cell and I am thinking, *I am going to die of cancer*. Will I go out bravely, seizing the day like they tell you, having the time of my life? That doesn't sound like me. Can I keep this a secret? I just want to die alone, without all that hovering and those sad, pitying looks. At least I can stop worrying about not going to the gym, and now I can eat all the ice cream I want. My mind is hurrying to pack all these thoughts in boxes for later. She is still talking.

I should ask questions. I am afraid to seem dumb. She assumes I know what she is talking about because I am a doctor. I interrupt her to say I don't know anything about malignant melanoma, so could she explain it, please? I can't be a doctor during this conversation. Now the dermatologist has stopped talking and my yellow page is full of sloppy blue ink because my hand has smudged the lines that slide down the right side of the page, and there are dashes and underlines I don't remember making. She asks where I want to have the "wide resection"; she names a cancer surgeon over in the local hospital, but I ask if I can go to the academic hospital in the city.

She says to call them today, "There is no use in waiting." I say, "Yes, I'll call them, today. Yes, good-bye. Yes, yes, thank you, thank you for calling."

Five minutes later a Google search brings me to the Melanoma Life Expectancy Calculator. I plug in my numbers and the biopsy result details from the yellow legal pad. The calculator tells me that I will die at age seventy-three. I have twenty more years. When did I think I would die? How old was Dad when he died? The calculator tells me that having melanoma will take two years off my life. Immediately I think—okay, 1996 and 2003, those were crappy years, good riddance, I will be happy to give up those years. I am terrified, but I laugh anyway, alone in my room with my diagnosis.

I arrive at the surgery building downtown at 5:45 a.m. and the room is already full, knots of three and four and five people waiting together. An empty reception podium stands by the double door. At 6:03 a woman with saddlebag hips comes out of an unmarked side door and in the voice of North Philadelphia asks, "Who's first?" It comes out as though she is speaking with a mouth full of sandwich, like "Hoooms-ferst?" She says out loud, to no one in particular, that people always know who's first, so just tell her—and she's right, we have all been keeping track. She tells the first group to *sit tight* or maybe she says *hold on*; I can't remember. On the panel TV nearest me a sleek and bald muscleman in workout shorts promises us, out of breath, that if we do the work, we can be transformed in ninety days. The North Philadelphia woman beckons to the first family, a group of six. Four adults stay seated while a man of seventy in shorts and white socks with new New Balance sneakers squeegees his way across the linoleum floor. His wife follows behind him in freshly ironed green Capri pants and pale-pink sling pumps. He looks pretty healthy. *What kind of cancer does he have?* I wonder. *Isn't this cancer surgery day?*

The second group is a couple. The woman is the one having surgery. She is in loose faded jeans and blue cork wedges. He is wearing the kind of striped polo shirt that men wear when they retire. The desk woman tells them her name is Erta and asks the woman if the man with her is her husband. She says no and laughs. "He's my friend," she explains. He looks in her eyes and puts his arms around her. Erta says, "Honey, he is more than a friend today. Today he is your significant other." Erta marries them right there at the desk using a white plastic wrist tag as a wedding band. They hold hands when they walk back to their seats.

Erta calls my last name: Robinson. I stand up and walk over. She looks at her paper and at her computer and at me, and at her paper, and asks for my birthday, saying, "People are going to ask you that all the time today." I tell her but I stumble and say the wrong year and then correct myself and say it again, twice. And Erta says "Yes, okay, honey, yes." Although I want to give her my left arm, she snaps the white plastic band around my right wrist. I am just about to reassure her by telling her I am a doctor when she says the next person I see will be a nurse and I can sit down now.

Twenty-five minutes later, a woman in sky-blue scrubs tugboats me though a pale-green hallway to Bay E3, where she docks me and pulls the curtain. I have become more obedient about my attire, and so I change into the hospital gown, cloth this time, white with blue piping, and a dark print of what—stethoscopes? At least it is not the paper kind, that pseudo-fabric made of crepe paper streamers like the one at the surgeon's clinic last week; that one ripped the moment I tried to put it on. This gown is a marvel of haberdashery with snaps and folds and ties and one-size-fits-all efficiency. I wrap it around me but don't bother with the ties. When I am a doctor, in the OR and in scrubs, I am always a bit modest, covered up with a T-shirt tucked into scrub pants, but this morning I don't seem to care. I am just a patient in a room. No one is really looking at me, and for a moment the anonymity frees me to be nervous or uncertain or silly; I can crack jokes or I can cry, because I have a pass today. I do not have to be in control of my face or my body or my emotions or my fear. The look I practiced for so long, the strong low voice, the serious eyes, they can all stay home this morning. I can sit here snapped up in my caftan of stethoscopes, the overweight bearded man in boxer briefs in Bay E3, the 9:30 a.m. case, here for resection of malignancy with local anesthesia. A patient.

Once the gown is on I sit in the chair in the cubicle meant for the family members I did not bring. A woman in the next cubicle is talking to a surgeon about her husband, who is a doctor, too, and she says, "Bring him back to me safe. Doctor, bring him back to me safe." And again, "Doctor, bring him back to me." No one in my family knows I am here. They live five states away, and I wasn't sure how to tell them about my diagnosis over the phone, at least not until I knew what I was facing.

My surgeon parts the curtain and walks in. He grips my hand with bony fingers and looks me in the eye for a moment, like I always do to my patients' parents, but his manner signals that he is in a hurry in a way that I hope is not so obvious when I do it. He is tall and thin and dark-eyed with a dark brown but smooth and irregular birthmark above his left eye. His short straight hair is turning gray. He calls me Mr. Robinson, and I do not correct him. He wants to mark the spot on my back he will cut out. I turn around in the chair, and he moves over and behind me. The starched edge of his white coat brushes my naked shoulder. I can smell the marker odor, and I know the ink is green though I cannot see it, and I can feel the cold wet circle he draws on my back. He comes back around to face me and asks if anybody is here with me, and I say *no*. His job is to mark the surgical site and meet the relatives so he can say something to them in the waiting room after the surgery is over. I wonder if he is glad I am alone. I think he wants to get away before I have the chance to say anything; we talked in his office last week, and that should be enough.

I wonder what he would have said to the family members I did not bring. Does he have a reassuring patter for them, like I do? Does he use his soft low voice? Does he lower his shoulders, sit down, speak slowly, take his hands out of his coat pockets, like I do when I talk to patients and families? Does he try to let the families borrow his confidence, like I do? This morning I don't want to talk about cell types and incision depth and prognosis and margins like we did in his office, but I want something more than nonchalance. I want him to say he'll stick with me, whatever happens in the next ninety minutes in that room on the other side of the hallway. As I am thinking all this, he says, "See you in a bit," and leaves.

A nurse in a dark-blue scrubs walks in and says his name is Brian. With great speed, he snaps up my hospital gown and ties all the cords in the back. He asks if there is anyone with me. Still no. He asks me to sit in the stretcher chair and pushes me out of the cubicle, down the green hallways and into Room 7. I was not expecting a full OR. I was not expecting a nurse to be scrubbed in. This is only local anesthetic—why is she scrubbed in? Why do they need a circulating nurse? This is a regular operating room; there is the glass-fronted cabinet with all the disposable supplies—the scalpel blades, curved and straight, organized by number and name; the sutures stacked in their neat boxes by size and color; the screw-top bottles of sterile water; the syringes, each in its own plastic sterile wrapper. There is the anesthesia machine, with its dashboard like a synthesizer, and the blue plastic tube hanging off the end near the black inflation bag and the vertical cylinder with the pump inside and the tanks strapped to the side, green and gray; there is the Bove machine with its off and on switch and the dial for turning up the cautery current. The room is set up as though this were serious. I try to figure out who is who, but no one looks at me or talks to me. What is happening? Why do they need the code cart? Why are they taking this so seriously? Am I really sick? I am grateful to get on the table, because now I can close my eyes, stay facedown, and imagine that I am somewhere else. Brian puts a sheet over me and straps me to the table.

I try to go over in my mind what will happen: the surgeon will remove an area of skin, blood vessels, nerves, and fat about the size of a deck of cards on the lower right of my back. Last week I took a picture in a mirror with my cell phone and saw what he would take—nothing special that I could see, just a biopsy scar.

Someone attaches leads to the back of my chest and puts an oximeter on my finger. The beeping machine picks up my pulse and my saturation. Over the next few minutes, the oximeter stops picking up my pulse and the beeping slows and deepens, but no one says a word. I imagine they are as practiced as I am at ignoring the beeping. But now the beeping is *me*, and it gets very slow and low-toned. Shouldn't someone react, someone other than me? All at once I think my heart will stop and my blood pressure will rise and I will stroke out and never leave this room because I did not say anything about the oximeter. Because I am a bad doctor who forgot something obvious and took or did not take my blood pressure medicines this morning and didn't I know not to do that? *What were you thinking?* they will say, and I will die on the table because I am a bad doctor who missed his own cancer and didn't bring anyone with me to the surgery.

I grit my teeth and squeeze my hands together. I wouldn't be thinking any of this if I were in scrubs and standing up. I would be calm and familiar, with my name tag hanging from my scrub shirt, checking my equipment or getting the forceps and sample containers ready, or supervising the fellow while she does it. I would be comfortable here in the OR, because after all this time giving bad news and heralding death and disease, the OR is a place of comfort for me, a place of control; no parents in the room, my skills sharp and efficient, my mind focused on the job. Before this morning, I liked the OR: no surprises, always help nearby if you need it.

Someone is washing my back with Betadine and then cold water, and my whole body is now draped and covered by the stiff blue sterile drapes. I hear the rustle of a sterile gown against the drape and I know that the surgeon is here, though he says nothing to me, as though he isn't aware I am awake. I feel the table being raised and I feel his waist against my side as he leans in close. He asks for Lidocaine with Epi and he announces, "This will sting and burn," to no one in particular.

He is right; it stings and it burns.

The surgeon checks my sensation with the end of a needle and I flinch so he injects more and I still feel the stick until I don't feel anything, not even the pressure of the needle. In my mind a perfect picture comes into view: First the scalpel cuts a smooth line into the skin, an oval incision with the knife, drops of ruby blood rising up from the cut edge in brilliant drops, the incision deepened by the cautery, white fat shrinking back from the electric blade and forming a faint grey edge, the blood receding from red and quick to black and still, the layers of tissue pulling apart as the incision goes deeper down until the red muscle is visible.

I wonder if I will smell my own blood and skin burning away. And then I do smell it, and I lie still and hold my breath.

Then I jump and say "Oh!" in a choked and tight voice. I am embarrassed and clench my teeth and back in fear and pain. A voice says, "Sorry, we're deep," and, "That was the muscle," and, "Another Lido with Epi, please." I wince and the drapes rustle again. I blame myself for flinching, worried that he will think I am a weakling, a silly doctor who cannot control himself, a stupid pediatrician. A voice asks for more Vicryl. I can't remember if that is the absorbable kind of suture for a moment, until I remember that it is.

Now the drapes come off and someone says, "I am putting steri-strips on," but I do not recognize the voice.

It's Brian, who tells me to stand up from the table. The surgeon is gone. The scrub nurse has her back to me doing the count and cleaning her table, and the circulating nurse is in and out and typing away on the computer keyboard; no one pays attention to me.

Brian puts me back in the gown and on the stretcher chair and wheels me out of the room past all the people walking about in the corridors. I do not look anyone in the eye on the way out because this time I am afraid of what my face will show; I can't see my face in my mind, so my expression is just what I feel, which is shaken and scared and relieved and nauseous and numb and angry and sad and relieved, everything all at once. Patients can show how they feel without thinking it through—it's allowed. I want to cry and cower under a soft quilt, sleep and dream and wake up in my own bed and not on this stretcher chair in these pale-green rooms and halls with fluorescent lights that stink of air freshener.

We take a wrong turn and end up in front of a locked wooden

door, but finally Brian deposits me in a different pod with a different nurse who takes my temperature and blood pressure. When she is finished, I ask if I can get dressed. She nods and I yank off the gown as fast as I can and get into my clothes.

I go across the hall to the bathroom and lift up my shirt to see the bandages on my back in the bathroom mirror. They are higher than I expected but clean and dry and white, lumped up gauze under three strips of white tape, with the light-brown stain of Betadine in a circle a few inches away from the bandage. I can smell the Betadine on my body and feel the pull of the tape when I raise my arm. I want to touch the bandage, to imagine how deep the cut was, to put my fingers in the wound to prove it is real. Like Thomas, I think I have to touch the wound to believe what has happened to the body, to know what is left. My face is pale in the mirror, and my sagging skin stands out like a wrinkled handkerchief. I feel old but alive, worried but alive, embarrassed and cold but alive, and out of place in a hospital bathroom for the first time in my life, awake and alive and slowly gathering myself up to go back out into the world.

Back in the pod I sign all the nurse's forms and take the prescription I will not use because I know acetaminophen will do the trick. Once we're finished she says, "Well, that's it. The exit is just down the hall on the right. Good luck, Mr. Robinson . . ." I am in my own clothes and mobile, still a patient but unconnected to the surgery by anything more than my white bracelet.

I open the exit door to see the waiting room again, but this time I have entered through an unmarked metal door on the far side of the elevators from Erta's podium. She is still there, reading the paper now, and the waiting room is less full, perhaps because the morning shift of patients has gone back into the OR, and Erta can relax with the Macy's ads until the afternoon schedule starts to fill up the room. The waiting room is brighter because of the risen sun, but the televisions still blare their ads and weather reports. Turning away from Erta, I walk down the white linoleum hallway and down the flight of stairs to the lobby of the building, where I take a seat for a few minutes on a white wire bench. I don't want to get in the car until I am calm.

So I just sit, watching the back and forth of people in the lobby, a three-story atrium of fake chrome and glass that could be the entrance to a shopping mall. Slowly I realize that I understand the people who walk by: this one is a resident, that one is a fellow, there is a nurse practitioner, an X-ray tech, three medical students, a woman in a wheelchair pushed by a nursing assistant, a cafeteria worker, a surgeon. There's a man with Marfan's syndrome—is he here for a coarct repair?—and there's a baby with a tracheostomy. Now I know where I am.

A six-year-old girl, brown hair in a ponytail and a white bandage across her eye—ocular muscle repair?—waits with her mother by the elevator to the parking garage, and I stand and go wait next to them. I look down at the girl and smile the smile I know works for sick six-year-olds, and it does: her lips rise a bit around the edges and her chin wrinkles. When the elevator comes, I hold the door for them. "After you, sweetie," I say with a generous wave of my hand. "You've got to move quickly with these hospital elevators. We're always in a hurry and you've been through enough today. Make sure you hold Mom's hand on the way down."

I am a doctor again.

My cancer now sits quietly under glass in a triptych of pressed cardboard in a file room in West Philadelphia, which, though I have never seen it, probably has fluorescent lights and gray metal shelves, with coded numerals at the end of every row: a library of removed human bits, preserved in case the cure does not take and we need to revisit the diagnosis. My cancer has moved around quite a bit in the last month; soon it will move to a storage facility, having traveled from the quiet real estate of my lower back through the hands of the surgeon to the clear plastic jar held by the nurse to the specimen basket at the main OR desk to the microtome room in Pathology, where it was thinly sliced and pressed between two rectangles of glass. Having determined that the margins had no visible cancer—though he did comment on the hair on my back, or so I read later in the report—the pathologist placed the slides in the cardboard tray for storage. The part of me not sliced thinly and preserved under glass has been incinerated at some other facility with all the other hazardous waste of the hospital, without ceremony.

Because I am a doctor again after the surgery, I know that my cancer sits in that pressed cardboard, and I know that the cardboard is greenish-brown like the algae in a brackish pond. Not because I have seen it, but because I have so often squinted through multiheaded microscopes at swirls of red-and-blue tissue on slides catalogued in the same type of container. I was looking at tissue I had snipped with a half-meter-long wire pincer from the newly transplanted lungs of a child in the same sort of operating room where I lay face down two weeks ago. In the lens I'd be looking for blue blobs surrounded by streaks of red close-by ovals of lighter red. I did not want to see a certain pattern in these slides. Not seeing this pattern would tell me that the child's immune system was ignoring the new lungs; we had fooled the body into a truce with foreign tissue, and the patient was a functioning hybrid of old body and new lungs.

In my microscope I was searching for a reassuring absence. Not seeing something and being reassured takes getting used to, but medicine has its own epistemic maneuvers, and I've learned through the years to believe the thing I did not see was not there. This is also my work as a patient: to trust that the unseen thing is not there at all, that more cancer is not hiding somewhere we did not look. Like the drunks and the lamppost, my surgeon and I decide to look only where the light is good. We are not going to look in my lymph nodes, we are not going look in my chest, we are not going to look anywhere but where we have already been. We decide to be reassured, and we will not meet again until we are proven to be wrong.

So I don't think about what's in my bloodstream, cancer cells that could be here or there floating along with my other cells and serum. I don't check my lymph nodes in bed at night. I don't think about being alone in the early morning on a plastic chair on the third floor of the hospital waiting for surgery. I don't think about being face down, wide awake, and all alone under stiff blue drapes in the OR; I try not to remember smelling the cautery burn my own numbed flesh. I think about other things. I think about the next twenty years, and about the memories of the sick children I have known, how I was a passer-by to their illnesses, how I intended to make things easier and better, but won't ever be sure if that is what happened. I wonder how the parents of the children I diagnosed remember me, if they do.

THE BOX AT THE BEDSIDE

Mucous from the lungs has a formal name—*sputum*—for research proposals and the medical chart, for reports to insurance companies or to referring doctors, but we will recognize it if you say *chest snot, hock-wads, loogies, lung boogers, lung-ers, snot-clots,* or *lung chunks.* If you are over fifty, you might call it *phlegm.*

Whatever you call it, sputum is my job. I inspect what is coughed up in tissues. I gaze into bedside specimen cups. I scrutinize the finer visual aspects of it: the color, consistency, and volume. I record its onset and frequency. And the sounds of sputum! Sputum production is the fanfare of lung disease, the low rumbly, wet raspy cough, the growling throat-clearing, the crowing-rooster, two-tone hacking when the soggy-sticky clump is just within reach, the tight-tired *blat* of a half cough half suppressed, the high musical wheeze of the dry cough that begs for the nebulizer—all these are the soundtrack of my work as a pulmonologist. I use the call-and-response of cough to make the diagnosis. The chorus of rough noise on auscultation points me to an area in the lung, upper or lower, right or left, while it tells me acute or chronic, if a chest X-ray is needed or not, whether to wait or to give steroids and antibiotics.

We usually keep all this to ourselves, we lung doctors, because we know that people don't want to hear about it. The coughs that interest us are disgusting to almost everyone. To the public a cough is something dirty and a cougher is someone to avoid. The public has been trained to hear the cough as a herald of communicable illness. Move over, cover your mouth, wash your hands, get away from me.

The tubercular cough has lost much of its currency these days, but it surfaces from time to time. We see it on-screen in *Moulin Rouge* when the delicate Flower of Art who yesterday swung trapeze-high from the ceiling swings low today, felled by the cruelty of a red-spotted handkerchief. In a Stephen King novel about a plague, we hear a single cough in a movie theatre, off to the side in the middle of the show, and this heralds the very certain death of the entire audience. That novel seems truer than ever in these days of a pandemic.

I am different: I cannot hear a cough without imagining the inside of the lungs, inflamed with fluid or oozing mucous, swollen and tight or loose and wet. Like the musician who hears music in birdsong and traffic noise, the pulmonologist, the sputum *specialist*, sees the X-ray and the mucous container in every cough.

A fourteen-year-old boy sits in a black T-shirt with angry white letters on the front, both hands gripping the game controller, twisting and shifting his body in the bed as the cars race ahead on the screen. His pillow is in its pressed case from home, a green-and-white pattern of small flowers. At his age, someone else is still doing his laundry. He wants the comforting pillow but has stopped bringing the matching sheets to the hospital, content to tolerate their institutional scratchy feeling, though he has not gotten to the stage where he can stand the cheap synthetic wool of the hospital blankets; he has a dark-blue comforter from home wrapped around his lower body, tucked under his right flank and draped over the end of the hospital bed. The video game monitor is on a stand on wheels at the left side of the bed, away from the door, so I can see the speeding, flailing race cars on the screen. His fingers, clubbed at the ends as they are in most people with cystic fibrosis, make soft clicking sounds against the controller's buttons, and he leans into the curves of the track with his body, riding the forces of gravity and the thrust of the virtual car here in the real world. His name is Mark.

The room temperature is turned down. All the other patients do this, though none of them can explain why they like it colder in the room or how they learned to do it; they haven't been allowed in each other's rooms in years out of fear of infecting each other with the germs in their lungs. I certainly don't mind the cooler temperature, because I always wear my long white coat over my white shirt and tie in the hospital, but the nurses complain, at least the newer ones do. The colder air is less humid, or perhaps the antibiotics make their skin flush warm, or perhaps they just like the sense of controlling at least one aspect of the room they are in.

In obedience to the infection-control rules, I am wearing a disposable thin plastic/paper gown made of a cross between the sort of paper we used to write on in kindergarten—the one with the bits of wood pulp visible and with a slippery oiled surface that made erasing your mistakes almost impossible—and the crepe banners the nurses hang on the walls for an inpatient's birthday. I am also wearing a blue face mask made of a similar plastic-paper hybrid, with a thin metal bar to pinch down over my nose so the mask fits; I have learned to pinch it and then pull it up a bit, so my glasses won't fog. These days everyone knows how to cope with glasses fog.

Gown, glove, and mask—it's the way we enter all the patients' rooms. Take it all off before you leave the room, leave any germs behind, say your prayers before and after with Purell, patients must stay in their rooms, no more pizza parties at night with the social worker, no more rap sessions, no more teen groups, no more play dates, no more summer camps. Everybody must keep their germs to themselves.

Although I knocked before I entered, Mark does not pay much attention when I come in. He knows I will come to see him every day at about the same time; he knows we will talk, and I will ask him how he is doing and listen to his chest, and I will look at his IV site and feel his belly. He knows I will ask him about his cough, about his sleep, about any headaches or rashes. He knows I will tell him about his lab results. He acts each day as though it is a deep imposition on him that I have come to see him, and he affects the air of an important businessman who is being bothered by a trivial matter, or perhaps a craftsman being interrupted in the middle of his work to be asked about the weather. And so he says only a low "hey" or "okay" when I stand by the bed and say, "Morning, how are you doing today?" His eyes never stray from the screen and his hands never leave the controller.

"Okay, let me see how you sound today," I say, flipping the stethoscope off its perch around my neck and pulling the earpiece calipers apart to set them in my ears. I place the round, flat end of the scope's head on the right side of his chest, just where the stretched neck of his T-shirt has slipped down an inch or two below his collar bone, pushing firmly down on the metal edges of the scope, and wait for him to take a breath. He doesn't, so I say, "Big breath in," and he obeys. I hear the whoosh of air enter his right upper lobe, a constant increase in the smooth sound of air flowing in the tubes of his airways, rising steadily in pitch like a quick glissando on a hoarse trumpet. Then I hear the gurgle at the end of the inhale, the sound of air slipping by something wet, a trumpet played into a bowl of mud. On the exhale, the sound is much louder, as the air is forced out by the contracting muscles of his thin rib cage—muscles grown powerful from years of coughing—and I hear only a slight whistling wheeze at the end of the breath, a plastic-penny-whistle sound for a second or two. I pick the scope head up off his chest, noticing the quickly fading pressure mark of the round metal and plastic disk on his thin and pale chest, and move the head of scope under the collar of his shirt to the other side of his chest. "One more time," I say, and on this side the trumpet is clear to the end, and there is no ending penny whistle.

"Got some stuff rattling around over here this morning," I say as I lightly touch the front right of his chest with my gloved index finger. "But the other side is clear."

Mark's eyes are still on the screen, fingers on the controller. If he has looked at me since I came in, it would have been when my eyes were on his chest or when I briefly closed my eyes to listen to his chest. Like him, I need to shut off the input from my senses sometimes, in order to pay better attention to what I am doing.

"Okay, let me listen to your back."

Mark exhales a faint grunt to signal his put-upon state. He leans forward, bent at the waist, eyes on the screen, torso still twisting with the G-forces on the screen. I too bend at the waist over his raised bedrail, and with my right hand I lift up the tail of his T-shirt, already damp with sweat and folded like a Japanese fan or the skin of an accordion's bellows, and slide my left hand with the stethoscope disk up under the shirt.

"Okay, big breaths again."

And we follow this rhythm, left to right, working our way in tandem down his back. I place the stethoscope head on his skin and he inhales and exhales on cue, and I listen and then move the head to another place on his back, six places in all. I close my eyes for a moment after each move, just after I press the disk onto his slightly sweaty skin and look up behind my eyelids, or cock my head to the left like a dog, listening to the movement of air in his chest.

At the bottom of his back, I listen and then say, "Okay, give me a big cough," and he does, a short, sharp inhale to something between a bark and a throat-clear, and I listen again to see if the gurgling sound on the inhale goes away. Then we do it again on the other side, two pairs of barks to see if the sound changes. As I stand back up I start to pull his T-shirt tail down, but he doesn't wait for me to get it back to where it was before. Maybe he likes the feeling of the cooler sheet against his bare skin as he reclines back on the bed.

"Okay, let me see your line," I say. Mark doesn't react as I pull up his right sleeve and look at the thin plastic line that dives into the crook of his arm through a hole in his body, the site covered in white gauze and a clear plastic covering like kitchen wrap with the date of the dressing change written by the IV technician in blue ink on the side. His arm is turned inward and angled so he can steer the car with the controller. I have to lean over the bed and twist myself around to see it. I don't want to interrupt his game yet. No redness, no swelling, no oozing; all is fine.

"Okay, Mark, so tell me, are you coughing a lot of stuff up?"

"Yeah, some." His attention is still on the screen, but he is listening to me as well, over the sounds of squealing tires and the cheers of the crowd.

"What's it look like, the stuff you are bringing up?"

His right hand twists the controller in the air, and the car on the screen slows down; after another moment he rests the controller on the bed, though his hands have not left the buttons.

"Can you show it to me?"

His hands leave the controller on the comforter and he turns to look up at me with a face of suspicion. "You *wanna* see it?"

"Sure."

He twists his right shoulder across his chest toward the bedside table. He has to shift back to the right for a second to pull at the line connecting his arm to the IV pole, and with more force he breaches up out of the sea of sheets like a whale, landing down on his left side enough to reach a round, white cardboard box on the table with his right hand. He twists off the slick white cardboard top of the box with the sort of movement a magician might use to reveal the card you picked out of the deck a few minutes earlier.

Inside the box is mucous he has been saving for me.

Here is the key to the mucous map: If clear to pale green and thin, all is well; keep doing the coughing exercises and chest physical therapy. If thicker and pale green, still okay, but more regular PT and regular inhaled antibiotics. If thick and dark green but still easy to cough up, add oral antibiotics; if not better after oral antibiotics, and still dark green and hard to cough up, IV antibiotics. If still not better, admission to the hospital.

And don't forget to look for blood. If specks of dark red, no problem; this is just swelling of the lungs and irritation of the lung lining with some oozing of the veins. If streaks of dark red, you are still probably okay; the blood has just clotted and darkened before you were able to cough it up. If bright red but just a few streaks, you are probably okay, but give us a call. If bright red and the size of a dime, call us sometime today. If bright red but less than a mouthful, call us right away; a weak walled blood vessel near an area of lung damage has burst. If bright red and more than a mouthful, go to the ER immediately and have them call us after you get there. If it's mouthfuls of blood and it doesn't stop, you probably won't make it alive to the ER.

No one can absorb all of this at once, and a person with a chronic illness has a lifetime of learning to read their body. And each person will be different, of course; as doctors we see scores of patients with similar problems, but each one can learn how to monitor their body in a unique way; we provide the wisdom of averages and broad experience, but the patient is wise in the ways of one body in particular. We need to have both sorts of wisdom in order to manage this disease.

Over the past day and night in the hospital, as Mark coughs during his chest physiotherapy—we all call it PT, where a therapist claps and pounds on his back while he coughs—or just any old time, he has been spitting what he coughs up into this cup, a clean white cardboard cylinder with a smooth processed surface so it won't absorb any liquid, and putting the cap of the box back on and keeping it on his bedside table. We told him to do this, not to swallow the mucous or spit it into a tissue, please. We want to dispose of it properly.

And we want to inspect it.

The floor of the box is stained a light yellow green, the color of new spring buds on a daffodil. Running down the edge of the sides of the cylinder in two or three places is the same sort of stain, where the mucous slid down the side as Mark held the container to his mouth to spit into it. On about two thirds of the bottom of the container, which is only three inches deep, globs of darker brown-green mucous sit immobile, moist centers in the middle of dried rims of mucous, like dark sunny-side-up eggs in a white frying pan. Sliding over and around these eggs is a thinner more translucent flow of pale-green fluid, slipping about in the container as Mark tilts the box with his practiced game-controller twist; this pale fluid slides over the dried-on egg lumps like thin lava flowing over itself, resisting the pull of the twisting gravity for a moment until the force gets too large and overcomes the desire of the stuff to cling to itself, and then it slides around and around the perimeter of the box like mercury in the bottom of a glass, a leading round edge followed by a trailing train of thinner liquid. Small specks of dried blood, dark brown and hard, dot the interior of the globs of mucous. One long strand of brighter red blood tangles and twists its way through the globs as they spin around in the bottom of the box.

Mark is watching my face, my eyes, my body. I do not move back an inch, but move forward and lean over to get a better look.

"Hunh," I say. "Looks lighter than yesterday, and really not any blood to speak of. What do you think?"

"Kinda dark, to me," he says. "But better than when I came in."

"When you're feeling good, at home, what does it look like, you know, on a good day?"

"I don't really look. It's gross."

"Hmm. But when you are getting sicker, you look at it, right? So you can tell when you need to come in, when you need to call us?"

"Sometimes. Yeah, sometimes, I guess. Yeah."

"Okay, good. So you think it's better than when you came in?"

"Yeah." Mark puts the cover back on the box and twists over to slide the it back on the bedside table.

"Is it easier to get it up, you know, during your PT?"

"Yeah."

"Okay, good. The antibiotics are killing the germs in this stuff, you know, your sputum, and all your coughing knocks it off the walls inside your airways, and you can get it up and out. That's how the antibiotics work. And when it gets darker and greener and thicker, that's when we need to use antibiotics, you know Cipro or something. If that doesn't make it better, you need to come in."

He looks at me, but his left hand is back on the game controller and he brings it over to his right palm. "Yeah, okay," he says.

He's waiting for me to leave. *Too much information*, I think, *too much all at once, too much teaching*. Time to go. Time to move on. *Pick up again tomorrow*, I think.

"Okay, well, let me feel your belly right quick now."

His eyes are back on the screen, and some twitch of his fingers has made the engines roar again. I lean over him and softly press on his abdomen; this isn't really the way to do it—he ought to be flat on the bed so I can get a good feel, he ought to have his abdominal muscles relaxed, the ones that are taut from all the coughing—but this is how it's going to go. If there were a problem, he would wince when I pressed, and he doesn't react at all. It will have to do. The visit is over.

"Okay man, well, anything I can do for you today?"

"Nah," he says, not looking up.

I put my hands on my waist on both sides to grip the yellow disposable gown as I turn toward the door. Halfway out, I pull off the face mask and toss it in the trash, turning to give Mark a full view of my unmasked face from the doorway as I say, "Okay, call me if you need me, okay?"

He nods but his eyes never leave the screen.

Two days after that first visit to Mark, I gown-and-glove up and knock on the door again. I haven't seen him over the weekend; the other doctors tell me he is doing better.

This morning he is on the bed with his laptop, watching something on it. He's still in the same black T-shirt, but he's taken a shower this morning and his hair is wet, slicked around on his head in spikes and casual waves that toss and land just so when he flicks his head. He's feeling better.

He turns to look at me as I come in.

"How are you doing today?" I ask.

"Ehh, okay," he says. His eyes wander back to the laptop screen.

"Still feeling a little better every day?"

"Yeah, pretty much."

"Let me take a listen," I say, and we go through the routine: "big breath . . . ," and the breath comes quicker now, the sound of the wetness gone; "big cough . . . ," and clear, none of the gurgle of a few days ago.

"You sound good," I say. "Antibiotics must be doing their job. And you're doing a good job with the PT, I hear."

"Yeah, well, I feel better."

"Good, good, that's the point, right?"

He looks me in the eye, *well, duh, dude!* flashing across his face. But there is something else, a smile, a bit of openness in his face, maybe some pride.

He reaches over to the table with his left hand, eyes still on the screen, but I think I see a smile breaking through. He holds a new round waxy cup, the product of his coughing for the last twenty-four hours. He's been waiting for this moment.

"Wanna see?"

"Sure," I say. "Show me what ya got."

WHITE CLOTH RIBBONS

Her face is gray in the darkening room. She rises up off the bed, clutching at the sheet, bending her body forward with the climbing pitch of every gasp, throwing herself back with each cough. Her half-empty open eyes scan down the bed. Now her head is back, her torso arched, and she's limp, head rolled over, jaw down, with long pauses between breaths, short and sharp hiccoughs of breath, noisy exhales. Sweat runs down her thin cheeks past cracked lips. She pants and gasps but keeps on breathing.

When she went into intensive care, everyone believed she would come out again; after two weeks, everyone began to doubt. The whole team listened to her chest and worked on her body. We increased every dose of every antibiotic, every mucolytic, every steroid, everything we could think of that might work. The most experienced clinicians came to her bedside in the last few nights and days. They tried everything. Nothing was working. This was it.

She must have known, when she was clearheaded, though I hadn't brought up dying to her. I wouldn't have known what to say. I was a first-year fellow in pulmonary medicine, and hers was going to be my first cystic fibrosis death.

Her family is here—two brothers, two sisters, and both parents. They are dressed in what they were wearing when they got the call to come: blue jeans, sweat pants, T-shirts or work clothes, a suit and tie. They've come from work or from school or from home; I don't ask. They've come because they got the call that now is the time.

They want to be here, but they do not know what to do. They have expected that her life would end, but she has survived so many other times in her thirty-five years, an eternity for someone with cystic fibrosis; they are used to the idea of the end, but still surprised that the time is now. No one knows where to stand, what to say, whether to whisper.

The room is dim and cold. The antiseptic pale blues and greens of the hospital room have shifted into gray or bright white. We have littered the floor under the bed with the plastic caps of syringes, the white-and-clear packaging of tubes and IV connectors and syringes. Alcohol swabs cut the stale smell of a small room filled with people. There are no flowers. Coats and sweaters and scarves cover the ledge of the radiator, and the trash baskets brim with translucent yellow isolation gowns, wadded and twisted into lumps and shoved down hard in the basket to make more room. The drapes between the bed and the glass door are closed. A yellow plastic bowl filled with thin wet tissues sits halfway on the bedside table. An IV pole bolted to the head of the bed holds three tan boxes blinking drip rates in yellow calculator numbers. Another two boxes, black and gray, cover the bottom of the bed below her feet, slowly pushing thick syringes full of clear fluids into the tangled IV tubing tracking up the bed toward the crook of her right arm.

She is dressed in a pink cotton T-shirt, one of the many from her collection of clothes brought from home so that she won't have to wear the scratchy hospital gowns; as they get dirty with snot and blood and spit, the nurses gently slide off the old one and pull a new one on over her head—nurses have been washing them every shift so that she always has something comfortable to wear. The white side of a blue plastic pad lies under her body below the waist. She is in a diaper because she has not been able to get out of bed for days. The nurses make everyone leave the room when they change it, and when everyone returns the bed is always smooth and clean, her hands resting quietly on the white cotton comforter, but she has not needed it changed for a few hours because her kidneys have shut down, and now the sheets and blanket are twisted and tangled with her struggle to breathe. Things won't be tidy again until the end.

We are all around the bed, the parents and the brother and the sisters and the nurses and I. I am alive to all the sounds of her cough, grading it against all the coughs I have heard in my past year of cystic fibrosis. All of us here know about coughs. Everyone in this room is used to the gurgle of the clearing throat; the low chesty rumble; the tight throaty growl other people can hear across two grocery aisles; the cough that keeps you from enjoying the last half of the play; the looser cough that signals success after a nebulizer; the short, sharp throat-clearer that gets you through the phone call. These coughs are all sounds that make a civilian look away and grimace, but no one here is a civilian.

It is the sound of this cough that drives the watchers at the bedside, the noise we follow more than the sights or smells. The sound right now is new, not the satisfying clearing cough, not the get-it-up-and-out kind, not the one that just needs a few more claps on the chest, not the one that finally clears with a nebulizer, not the one that bring tears but relief. This cough is cut short, a gurgling churning noise that catches in her throat and slides back down into her swollen lungs, followed by a lower chugging rasp that is just the sound of air and mucous.

This is the sound that drives the watchers mad.

An hour ago she woke up; she saw her family around the bed, all in the room. She saw her brother and her sister. She said, It's bad, it's bad. She said, I love you, I love you all. They said, We love you, too. They all kissed her. They all held her. They all looked right into her eyes and said it again, we love you, we all love you, precious darling, we love you. And then she drifted back down, sliding past them downstream into the bed, her body slipping into the pillows and sheets.

She stiffens with each breath, her jaw out, neck muscles tight, shoulders shrugged forward. Each breath finishes with a little gasp. The cough no longer grips her body. Her breath is a shallow splashing sound, not yet a choke. Her mouth is open, lips cracking, gray. Broken capillaries and not enough oxygen blue-black her face and yellow her eyes.

We leave the room, the parents and I. They say, Can't you help? I list the things we are doing, the medicines. I say we are already on ceftaz, tobra, and vanco. And we are already on colistin. And the levels of tobramycin and vancomycin in the blood are good. And we already added more pulmozyme. And we can't use imipenem, remember, she's allergic. We are doing everything but nothing we are doing is working. The CO_2 marches up. It is the highest I have ever seen, I tell them. I say, I do not think she is going to survive.

They ask me, Can she feel it? Does she know?

I say, I do not know what she is feeling, but I think she can hear you, I think she knows you are here and that you love her, but she is not really here, she is somewhere in-between. And I do not know how long that will last.

This is what I need to say: There's no point in giving more morphine. She is already on so much morphine to calm her cough that adding more is pointless, and the last few doses have made no difference anyway; everything that morphine can do has been done. I can use something different, a different drug that doesn't fight coughing or pain but would make her relax. But if she relaxes, if she stops fighting so hard, she might die.

I do not want to say that I am afraid the medication to make her relax might kill her. I want to speak in a low voice that will sound calm, lay out all the facts, be the doctor, the one who knows. But I don't know. Anybody who says they know what she is feeling or what her life is like right now is making it up. I know I want her struggle to be over. I want her to be calm, but I do not want her to die because I give her more sedation. I want it to be over for her, but I do not want her to die that way. I want to make her calm, floating along and away, not clawing and scratching for what is left of life. I want her body to stop its animal struggle to stay in the living world. I want her to drift slowly out to the horizon to wherever people go, to somewhere without coughing and hospitals and IV lines and lung graphs, somewhere she never has to meet me, someplace where we are strangers standing in line for a movie and I am not in charge of her suffering.

This is true as well: I want it to be over for me. I want it to be over, one way or the other. Not in-between. I want it to be like on TV: the soft forgiving shudder of a life slipping out the door, the slow angelic fade to a commercial, the quiet bloodless exit of a soul to some better place so that afterward the family and the doctor can live with themselves, knowing they did all the right things and her life was worth it. I want to cue the montage of her happier times in a sunny park as the camera slowly pans up the hill to the cemetery. I do not want stand here and watch her fight and claw and gasp her way into the next scene. I do not want to be the doctor who heads for the elevator, like the others have, but I also don't want to be the one who stands by doing nothing. I want to be the doctor everyone remembers for being kind and courageous, not the one who wrung his hands at the bedside. I do not want to kill her, but I want her to go ahead and die, for it to be over, for myself and for her and for her family. I do not want her to struggle and suffer. In a lifetime she has suffered enough. There is no point in any more, but who am I to say so?

Her parents are stronger and clearer than I am. Her parents have more practice at life than I do. They ask me, Isn't there something, some medicine that will make her relax? They say, Give the medicine to make her relax. They say, We can't let her be like this. We know it is the end. We love her, with all our hearts. We have known this was coming. They are holding hands. They are stronger than I am. They say, Give her the medicine. We know what the medicine might do, we know what you can do, doctor.

And so I give the smallest dose I can give, the smallest one in the smallest syringe slowly flushed in through her IV. Over ten long minutes, her face relaxes. Her mouth still hangs open, but the gurgling sound is softer. Her breathing is softer. Her face is still. Her hands relax. Her eyes do not change; they are half open, staring down the room. She does not rise off the bed. Everything seems softer in the room: the light, the smells, the sounds. We are all breathing slower and quieter. We are all watching.

Her family holds her hands and kisses her forehead. They say good-bye over and over. They say, We love you, honey. They say, Go on, it's okay. It's all okay, honey. We are here. You can go. We love you.

She keeps slowing down, and the room slows down with her. Her body sags now. She stays settled into the bed's wrinkled spaces. For a while she still twitches with each breath, but as the minutes pass the twitch becomes a shrug and then a sigh and then even less. Her head falls to the side, mouth still open. Her eyelids are dull white, her hair dry, her hands cooler. The sun is coming up behind the curtain. The family is watching now, not listening. We have shut off the monitors.

She does not breathe for over a minute by my watch, and then little upward gasps, all neck muscles. And then no breath for two minutes, and then none for four. Her face is dark pearl gray, dull with no more hint of blue. Her hands are cold. I lean over and place my stethoscope on her thin chest, pressing hard on her cool skin and feeling the round head of the scope rock back and forth against her thin ribs; I listen, feeling heavy with the effort, closing my eyes so I can hear the smallest sound of the briefest heartbeat. Everyone in the room is quiet. I open my eyes and look at my watch and keep listening. Slowly, knowing everyone's eyes follow me, I stand back, take the earpieces out with both hands, and flip the scope over my shoulders.

I think it's over, I say. One more look at her half-open eyes, my hand on her thin shoulder. Yes, it's over. She's gone. My voice is low and sure, my eyes are dry, and my chest is empty.

I back away from the bed, and the family flows in to take my space. There is no need for me here now that I have spoken my last lines. But my job is not over—there is paperwork to do. I need to tell the nurses upstairs, though they have been in and out of the room all night, their minds in that room with us while they tended to the needs of the living, and now they must tell those in-patients, the ones with the same disease who know her and know she is in the ICU, that she is gone. I don't know if any of them are surprised, or if they ask how it went, or if they ask who was the fellow in charge. I imagine that they will look at me differently, at least all the older ones, when I see them later today. I imagine everyone will look at me differently now, but I don't know if that will be true because there are so many deaths and so many patients and so many families and so many rooms where life just ends. No one in the ICU even notices me. People die there all the time.

I pull out the paperwork from the file labeled "Death Kits" in the nurse's station and get to work. I send the paperwork down, but then I have to speak to the administrator on duty because I have done the death certificate wrong: I have used black ink and it has to be blue or I have used blue and it has to be black, I can't remember, and I have listed the wrong cause of death, because cystic fibrosis cannot kill you on a death certificate, she says; only respiratory failure can kill you on a death certificate. I fill out the form again. I write the last note in her chart, describing what happened and what I did.

I go back in the room once the family has gone. We keep the drapes to the hallway closed but open the shades and turn on the lights. We move the chairs out of the room back into the hall. We are quiet, but we are not whispering. The sun is coming into the room through the dirty window, and the dull winter morning sun makes us squint, but we do not close the blinds.

The nurses have already taken off her T-shirt and the diaper and pushed the sheets and blankets down into a pile at the foot of the bed. Her naked body seems too small in the middle of the length and width of the bed, and she is sunken down into a divot in the white field of the bottom sheet. Her head is rolled over to the left. The end of the IV lines are still taped into her arms and chest, because, the nurse tells me, we are not supposed to remove them in case of an autopsy. I know there will be no autopsy. Her torso and legs are a solid marble white, blank and dense and floppy, but her arms are marked with the yellow-and-blue bruises of previous IVs; I am surprised the bruises look the same against the gray skin—they do not need warmth or a pumping heart to keep their color. Her fingers are awkwardly curled under her hand and her left wrist is flexed in a way I think must hurt until I remember, but still I reach out to straighten them. The nurses have gotten warm water and washcloths and I help clean off her legs, feeling useless but wanting to be there to help the nurses if I can. The senior nurse teaches me how to open the death kit to get out the plastic draping, the slippery white wrap that fits around the body. Using the blue plastic pad, I roll her body sideways toward me while the nurse bunches the plastic wrap under the body/ As I let her body roll back toward the nurse's side of the bed, I pull out the blue pad and grab the edge of the white plastic, pulling it toward me and sliding her whole body toward me at the same time; then with me at her feet and the nurse at her head, we pick her up and line up her body on the middle of the bed, with equal flaps of the white plastic on either side of the body. She isn't heavy but she is hard to move, since her body now has none of the expected solidity of the living bodies I have lifted and moved: it's like trying to push an uncoiled rope.

The nurses begin to wash her face with a white washrag and brush her hair with a blue plastic brush that comes in the death kit. We arrange her in just the right way, silently making little adjustments to her body and to the slippery draping. I tie the white cloth ribbons around her feet to hold them together and around her wrists to hold them across her chest. We fold the bottom edge of the plastic sheet up over her feet and the top edge down over her head so that the hem rests at about her collarbones. We fold the right side of the white plastic over her, covering her whole body and head, and make tiny adjustments until the edge is straight and tucked just so under the left side of her torso. Then the left side, and we hold the edge of the slippery plastic tight against the weight of her body, rolling it to the left; we pull the sheet taut and tuck it under her. We fold and wrap and straighten some more, and we tie the longer cloth ribbons tightly to the outside of her body to make a sealed package. We work until we have gotten it right, until her body is safe and secure in the wrapping.

We strip off all the sheets and the blankets and stuff them down into the red bin. We pull the filled bins out of the room into the hallway and put all the monitors and IV machines on a rolling cart to be sent down for cleaning.

The nurse calls the morgue technician, and he comes up the back elevator with the key, bypassing all the floors so no one else can get on. He brings the stretcher with the green canvas top, the one with the frame inside to hold the cloth in a rectangle so you cannot see the shape of the body. We pick her up and move her over to the stretcher, holding the white plastic wrap tight. The technician puts on the frame and cover and wheels her away. A woman in a blue-striped housekeeping shirt comes in pushing a wide yellow broom under the bed to sweep away the debris, getting the room ready for the next patient, and I head downstairs for morning rounds.

THE KISS OF SALT

Six people are waiting for a diagnostic test on a bank of green plastic benches in the hallway of the Pediatric Lung Clinic in 2005: a mother and a father, two grandmothers and one grandfather, and a five-week-old boy. Until an hour ago, the baby was wrapped up against the cold New England winter, but now he is sleeping in his mother's arms in a pale-blue onesie. All the adults are listening for the baby's name to be called. No one in the group is talking. The mother is gently dancing the baby in her arms, though from look on her face I doubt she even knows she is moving. The father sits one grandmother away from the mother and baby. He is quiet, scanning the hallway with his eyes, looking carefully at the other families as they walk by. The grandmothers seem to share the same face, third-generation Irish ladies in Boston, pale with a hint of pink lipstick and pale hair in short curls, each in a blouse suitable for meeting someone new. The lone grandfather has a dark button-down shirt on under a green wool sweater. All the adults' parkas are in his lap, and his thin frame is swallowed by their bulk. Two large quilted blue bags compete for space on the floor with the ten assembled feet. Without looking inside I know that the bags are bloated with diapers, bottles, cleaning towels, extra baby clothes, and those large plastic keys people love to shake at babies, the things that a first-time mother thinks she needs every time she leaves the house; she was distracted this morning so there will be something forgotten, something she will wish she had tucked in the bag at the last minute.

I walk by them just as I walk by other families in the hallway. In my white coat with a stethoscope slung around my neck, I get their momentary attention, and I might have smiled, I don't remember. Every new mother in a specialist's clinic thinks the unknown doctor walking down the hall might be *the* doctor. Every new father in the clinic is scanning for the doctor with the answer. But until the test results are in, I am just a stout man in a white coat, so I walk on past the bench-sitters. As I always do when I pass new parents in this hallway, I think: I hope you never have to meet me.

The test they have come for is an odd one, full of history but so unusual that almost no one has heard of it: the "sweat test," an assay for the amount of salt in the sweat of the baby. The test is to diagnose cystic fibrosis, and it will be positive in one of every thirty-five hundred white babies in the United States. The public knows CF as a killer of children, but the public is wrong. Cystic fibrosis today is a life-limiting but chronic illness, along the model of type 1 diabetes, something that will shorten your life but that you can manage with hard work. Most infants diagnosed with cystic fibrosis today survive into their forties. But the people on the bench don't know that, and they must sit with their ignorance for the time being. The letter from their pediatrician said the blood test done when the baby was born was "positive for cystic fibrosis," although it was just a screening test; the real diagnosis would come from what happened today, though their doctor didn't have the time to explain this very well and just gave them the number of our clinic to call. So they called, and they came in the next day, and they are next up for the strange-sounding test for a disease they had never heard of before.

Most parents won't remember signing permission for the newborn screening. An about-to-be father and a laboring mother would sign any form a nurse put in front of them, especially one in eight-point type and covering several pages. Who wouldn't agree to a test to make sure everything is fine with the baby? And so when the baby was brought back into the tired mother's room with a tiny round band-aid on his heel, the only question they ask is: Who would be so mean to stick a newborn baby's heel for blood? The nurse explains: He'll be fine, it's all okay. It's just the screening tests. We do it on every baby. Don't worry. The screening tests are forgotten in the rush of learning how not to drop the baby, how to care for the still-damp umbilical cord stump and the yellow clamp attached to it, how to burp and feed the new family member. There are worries enough in the first month of life. And so the letter from the pediatrician's office comes as a bolt from the sky. Positive for what? they say. What does that mean? There is no disease in our family! The pediatrician said the baby was fine! They have been on the internet. They have read the disease description on Wikipedia, and the blogs of the mothers of children with CF. They have read the words *fatal disease* more than once and enough for a lifetime. They have cried and worried; they have told some people but kept it secret from others; they have told the grandparents in phone calls and face to face, and the grandparents have fueled their worries with stories of their own about this disease, stories of a thin child in a primary school class who didn't make it, stories of someone from church who had a niece with this, stories they blurted out without thinking, stories they wish they had kept to themselves. And now everyone is here in the clinic, on the edge of this bench, waiting to be called for the test.

There is a line of these families sitting in our clinic hallway every day, newborns in arms, either waiting for the sweat test to be done or waiting for the results. Every family is an amalgam of fear and defiance. The scared ones, like these, don't talk much, but the look in their tired eyes is clear: our dreams are at risk. The defiant ones are sure the test is wrong. They've never heard of this disease, there isn't any disease in our family, the baby looks fine, *our baby is fine.* About half of them have read that babies with cystic fibrosis taste salty when kissed, and they have been kissing the baby's forehead every now and then to see for themselves.

For this family, the test will begin in a few minutes. A bald man of about seventy in a long white coat will call their name in his heavy accent—he comes from Iran, but says he is Persian, "because it was Persia when I left it"—and then escort them into a small room off the main hallway, "just Mother and Baby, please; come right in, Mother, it is all okay." His name is Dr. Abbas Mahmoodian and he has been working in our clinic for decades, longer even than the division chief; he is what you might call a fixture, and these days all he does are sweat tests. Dr. Mahmoodian calls all mothers Mother and all babies Baby. He pays little attention to anyone else, but he is a kind and gentle man. He has been doing this so long on such a parade of mothers and babies that he can't feel too worried for any single Mother and Baby until the test result is in. And anyway, most of them will be normal. Dr. Mahmoodian's accent seems to emerge more strongly for the happy news he usually tells me over the phone, "Nohrr-muhl, Dr. Rob-bean-son. No worries; Baby is nohrr-muhl."

Dr. Dorothy Andersen was traveling in August 1948, out of the heat of Manhattan. She wasn't at her cabin in New Jersey, and she didn't come into her office in the pathology department on 165th Street until after the heat wave had passed. So it was news to her that some of the children in her cystic fibrosis clinic had been brought to the hospital for dehydration on Friday, August 27, and Saturday, August 28; the temperature had topped 100° F on those two days, and five children from the cystic fibrosis clinic were admitted to "Babies" (as Columbia Presbyterian Babies' Hospital was called by everyone in the city) that weekend. Both babies were given the diagnosis of heat prostration and dehydration. When she returned to work, she must have been told about the admissions, but there is no evidence she took them seriously. It was very hot, and little children get dehydrated in hot weather, especially if they are too young to ask for water or to get it themselves. Sick children are more vulnerable than healthy ones, and things happen to them that don't happen to a healthier sort of child. The cystic fibrosis children both recovered and that was the end of it.

Until it happened again. The next summer, 1949, two more children in the cystic fibrosis clinic were admitted for dehydration, and this time their lab work startled Dr. Andersen. These children had a peculiar form of dehydration. The sodium and chloride levels in the blood were low, not high. Usually, a child dehydrated due to hot weather loses more water than salt in the sweat, and so the concentration of these ions in the body should increase, not decrease. But the cystic fibrosis children seemed to be losing both water and salt. And oddly, sweat had been dripping off these children at the time of admission, a remarkable thing in a dehydrated child whose body should be trying to conserve water, not leak it out through the sweat glands.

Dorothy Andersen was already famous in 1948 for having discovered a disease she called "cystic fibrosis of the pancreas." Ten years earlier she published a case series based on characteristic scarring in the pancreas seen on autopsy in infants and young children. Her lecture at the American Academy of Pediatrics meeting on May 5, 1938, entitled "A New Variant of Celiac Disease" and her subsequent paper in the *Journal of the Diseases of Children* in August of the same year had described a variant of "celiac syndrome," a catch-all term used then to indicate a trio of symptoms in children: failure to grow, a distended abdomen, and attacks of diarrhea with large, pale, and very foul-smelling stools. In the years since the publication of her first report, scores of case reports of similar children had been published, and children from all over the East Coast had been referred to Andersen for diagnosis and treatment. By 1948 Andersen and her colleagues were following at least sixty-five children diagnosed with the new disease, now common enough to be shortened to cystic fibrosis, or just CF, at Babies Hospital, and even more had been seen in which the diagnosis was suspected but not confirmed.

Making the correct and specific diagnosis was important because by 1948 Andersen and her colleagues had the beginnings of a treatment regimen. She treated the children by instituting changes in the diet to decrease the frequent stooling, adding an old therapy of ground-up pancreatic extracts with every meal, and the children began to gain weight and grow again. The nutritional therapy was founded on an educated guess based on what was already known about the pancreas: one part secretes insulin into the blood stream, and the other secretes digestive enzymes that break down fat in the duodenum, just past the stomach. Only the area of the pancreas that produces digestive enzymes was damaged on the autopsy slides of the children who had died, and damage in that area had been associated for decades with excessive fat in the stool. So changing the diet and replacing the pancreatic enzymes was a good idea, and when she tried it, it seemed to work.

Andersen also began to use newly available antibiotics to treat the pulmonary infections that these children were prone to developing. Early on, only the sulfonamides were available, but once World War II ended, penicillin was available for civilians, and Andersen and colleagues began using it for the lung infections seen in these children. For many of them, the treatment was miraculous. Their cough decreased or disappeared, and they began to grow and thrive. No one knew why the pancreas and the lungs were affected in these children. No one knew what caused the disease. Andersen had some theories, but all she really knew was that these children had a certain cluster of symptoms—failure to gain weight, greasy stools, and sometimes cough—and the treatment was based on educated guesswork rather than an understanding of exactly what was wrong in the child's body.

As the number of children referred to her increased, Andersen needed an accurate method of diagnosis so her new treatment could be used on the right children. She had first described the disease by recognizing a characteristic pattern in autopsies, but the pancreas could not be safely biopsied in a living child; what she needed was a way to make the diagnosis when treatment could make a difference. Was there a way to test whether the pancreas was secreting digestive enzymes into the intestine? A tube passed through the mouth and down past the exit of the stomach, near where the pancreas emptied, could collect samples of the fluid secreted by the pancreas. If there were no digestive enzymes in the sample, then she could conclude that the pancreas was damaged, and she could assume the child had the new disease. The test was available, but performing it was hardly simple.

An educational film about cystic fibrosis from 1956 shows part of the duodenal tube aspiration test being performed. An adult male narrator announces, "Another problem in diagnosis has been the difficulty of performing adequate tests. Here's Martha, demonstrating the duodenal drainage test, which is uncomfortable for the patient and difficult for the doctor." A four-year-old girl—I have no reason to doubt her name really is Martha—lies uneasily on a gray examination table, her white cotton underwear pulled up over her protuberant belly and her thin legs stretched out flat. Every time I see the film, I feel sorry for Martha; to my experienced eyes four decades later, she not only clearly has CF but is already a very sick girl.

In the film the tube has already been placed down Martha's nose and esophagus into her stomach and then out through the pyloric valve into the first part of her duodenum. Martha is supine on the stretcher and breathing heavily even though she is at rest. Her lung disease is already advanced. We can see her barrel-shaped chest rise and fall with each breath; her lips are closed tightly, and her dark-brown hair is swept back off her face and onto the white sheet of the examination table, as though someone has been stroking her hair or wiping sweat off her forehead. The brown rubber hose exits from her right nostril, held in place by a mustache of thick white tape. Her chin is resting on her chest, and we can see her ribs with every breath. The tube flops down into her left armpit and touches the inside edge of her bent elbow before diving off the edge of the table and then looping back to be held by tape and a safety pin to the white bedsheet. The end of the rubber tube rests in a glass test tube taped to the same safety pin. About a tablespoon of translucent, yellow fluid sits at the bottom of the tube.

Martha has her arm raised up at the shoulder and her elbow bent with her left hand near her hair above her ear. Her face broadcasts her determination to endure. She knows she must not move, must not touch the tube or her nose. A hand reaches into the frame from the left and grasps Martha's head between its thumb and forefinger, turning her head to the right. The frame shifts in for a close-up, and we can better see Martha's sallow skin and pale lips. She has dark circles under both eyes. The camera follows the trail of the tube from her nose down to the test tube as the narrator explains the point of the test.

Martha's face is eloquent in its restraint: she will endure the test, but there is something expectant in her grimly tight mouth and her steady gaze at the ceiling. We can imagine she has had this test before, because the filmmakers and doctors want to show a positive test, and undergoing it again for the film has pushed the boundaries of her patience. She does not turn to look at the camera, even though the process of being filmed must have been new to her; she is holding still and being good. She must be hungry, since any test involving putting a tube down the throat of a child goes better for the doctor on an empty stomach. The film does not show the tube's removal, but I know it would have been as unpleasant as its placement. Pulling off the thick, sticky tape mustache would pull the skin of her lip into an uncomfortable pinch, and removing the tape would replace her white mustache with a red one of irritated skin; then she would feel the slow and steady tug on the tube, the feeling of it ascending in her throat, the sudden arrival of the need to retch would vanish the instant the tube is out. There would be involuntary tears after it was all over, not from fear but from having her nose lining scraped, though I imagine Martha might be irritated by her body's betrayal. Such a tough child, and accustomed so young to the rough work of doctors.

We do not see any of this, so we do not know whether Martha was able to maintain her gritty sang-froid during the off-screen parts of the test. Martha cannot tell us now: even with the best possible care and luck, a girl her age in 1956 with cystic fibrosis who already had enough lung disease for me to see it just by looking could not have survived more than a few years after the filming was done.

Back in the small room off the clinic hallway, Dr. Mahmoodian is busily preparing for the sweat testing. Mother and Baby are in a green hard-plastic chair pushed against the wall.

After telling Mother in a gentle and firm voice to hold Baby's hands, he cleans a two-inch square space on the surface of the baby's inner wrists with alcohol and paints a clear solution on the baby's skin in these areas. He then places a small square of cotton gauze over each square and seals it down with plastic wrap and tape. It is only then that Mother notices the gray box with dials and wires to her right sitting on a small table under the window. It has the look of a homemade Ham Radio: two switches on the front, a meter with a fine needle resting all the way over to the left of a dial, and a battery hooked up to the box with black wires. Dr. Mahmoodian wraps two rubber straps around both of Baby's arms, one on top of the gauze and one below it. The straps hold a flat, gray metal plate with a small knob in the middle of it to the surface of the baby's skin. Dr. Mahmoodian gently reminds the mother to hold the baby tight: "It is important for the testing, Mother, to hold Baby still, please." He reaches over to the gray box and takes two wires in his hands, each with one red and one black alligator clip on the end. He attaches the clips with the black wire to the post over the gauze and the clips with the red wires below the gauze on each arm and flicks on the silver switch on the box.

The needle jumps into action. Baby does not react.

Dr. Mahmoodian says, "Now hold still, all will be over in a minute."

After a few minutes Dr. Mahmoodian pulls the clips off the posts, undoes the rubber straps, checks that the plastic wrap is secure around the gauze, and says, "It is mostly over, Mother. You wait in the hall. I will call you." He turns the dial on a kitchen timer and stands up, ushering Mother back to her seat on the bench with the rest of the family.

She sits back down on the end of the hallway bench, this time next to her husband, and begins to explain to her family what just happened. They know the test is almost over and the baby is now calmly sleeping. What they do not know is how lucky this baby is compared to Martha. What they do not know is that what just happened to Baby was the was the direct result of Dorothy Andersen's investigation of the dehydrated children with cystic fibrosis during the heat wave in the late 1940s. All they know is that life may change forever in about half an hour.

The story of the dehydrated children nagged at Andersen. What did it mean for the new disease? Perhaps the sweat glands were blocked just like the pancreatic glands, and so the children could not sweat enough to cool their bodies down. Inability to sweat could cause the heat prostration. But the inability to sweat did not match the clinical picture—it would raise the salt levels in the blood, not lower them, and besides, the children were covered in sweat in the emergency room, sweating more than they ought to have been. The sweat glands could not be blocked.

A second theory flashed in her mind: Could the children have a metabolic problem that made them sweat too much? Andersen knew that in the early 1940s the families of several children diagnosed with cystic fibrosis had moved out of New York to warmer climates in the hope of avoiding respiratory infections. But some of these children had died after the move, and the ones who survived did not thrive, though Andersen did not have detailed information on what had happened to them. Could an inability to stop sweating in a heat wave cause the children to become dehydrated? Usually, the body will conserve the fluid in sweat during dehydration, no matter how hot it is. Maybe these children couldn't do that, and so they kept sweating and sweating until they were dried out? At least this theory matched some of the clinical details of the children in the emergency room.

Andersen set one of her junior colleagues, Paul di Sant' Agnese, on the trail of the dehydrated children. Di Sant' Agnese was an Italian physician who had come to Columbia in 1939 for further training and had been chief resident in pediatrics. He had done impressive work on the neurotoxin-based paralysis associated with some tick species, and he had become interested in celiac disease as well as other inherited metabolic disorders. On finding that a colleague at Columbia had a constant-temperature room—basically, a room with a reliable heater and an accurate thermostat—and a method to collect sweat on gauze pads stuck onto the back, he took what he later called a "shot in the dark" to study sweating in patients with cystic fibrosis. He selected two healthy teenagers without cystic fibrosis as controls and two of a similar age with the disease and tested the sweat volume and salt content after a time in the hot room. In the healthy teens, as expected, the sweat contained some salt. In a healthy human, sodium chloride is excreted with the sweat at about a hundredth of the concentration of the sodium in the blood. The difference in the teens with cystic fibrosis was immediately clear: they produced a much higher volume of sweat and had ten times the expected amount of sodium and chloride in their sweat.

No wonder the children with CF had become dangerously dehydrated. They were losing fluid and salt in the sweat at a much higher rate than the healthy children. Di Sant' Agnese was a careful researcher, and so he repeated the procedure with a group of fifty children with cystic fibrosis compared to sixty children without the disease, looking for other possible explanations for the high salt content of the sweat. Still the answer was the same—the children with CF had a higher volume of sweat and a much higher concentration of sodium and chloride in the sweat.

Yet di Sant' Agnese suffered a crisis of confidence in his findings. No physiologist had ever described excess salt in the sweat. No explanation for the increased salt presented itself. Without a potential physiological explanation, or even a plausible theory, the results might be a mistake, no matter how many times he obtained the same result. When he presented his results to an audience at Columbia that included the eminent Japanese physiologist Yas Kuno, author of the authoritative text *The Physiology of Human Perspiration*, the reaction was exactly what he feared: Dr. Kuno listened to the paper in stony silence in the second row. At the end of the talk, Kuno rose slowly and said a single word: "Impossible." The others at the conference agreed: The salt concentration could not have been as high as di Sant' Agnese reported; the measurements were off; the controls were wrong; the room temperature was inconsistent; the skin was contaminated. No theory of sweating could account for the values found on the skin of the patients with cystic fibrosis, so the facts must be mistakes, no matter what the measurements showed.

Di Sant' Agnese pressed forward, encouraged by other colleagues around the country who were eager for an easier physiological test for cystic fibrosis than the pancreatic tube method. He presented his data on the difference in sodium and chloride in the sweat of children with CF at a lecture for the May 1953 meeting of the American Pediatric Society in Atlantic City. After the talk, di Sant' Agnese recalled, there was not a single question or expression of interest from the audience. He was unsure if this meant that no one disagreed or that no one cared, but the answer was that what had been so controversial among the physiologists seemed perfectly plausible to the clinicians, who were perhaps more accustomed to uncertainty than their scientific colleagues.

The breakthrough of a measurable physiologic difference separating children with CF from healthy children represented a substantial shift in the way doctors thought of cystic fibrosis. The sweat anomaly suggested that CF was a systemic illness, not just a failure of one or two organs, and that the disease must have a mechanism that affected the entire body in some way. A disease that had been diagnosed by symptoms or by specific organ damage seen on autopsy was now a disease that could be diagnosed by a physiologic measure even in the absence of clinically evident symptoms. If the difference in the sweat of those with and without CF was true, couldn't there be people without symptoms who "had" the disease, even though they had no symptoms yet? Wouldn't this new test be a way to screen infants for the disease even before they developed symptoms? In any case, sick children kept presenting themselves to the clinic for diagnosis and treatment, and the need for a reliable test for diagnosis was pressing the clinicians.

What di Sant' Agnese needed now was a reliable way to collect and analyze sweat from children suspected of having the disease. The controlled-temperature research room was a rarity; an easier method had to be found. Researchers around the country looked for alternatives over the next few years. Almost every accessible bodily product that could be tested was a candidate to be examined for excess sodium chloride, from stool (no good—too variable due to diet) to urine (no good—no excess salt is secreted here) to fingernails (again, no good—too dry to analyze) to tears (no good—too hard to collect reliably) to ear wax (no good—no excess salt detected). It would have to be sweat, and there would have to be a way to collect and analyze it.

In the 1956 film, Martha again demonstrates one test under consideration. The duodenal test demonstration is over, and now Martha sits upright, looking directly at the camera, sulky but curious. We see her small hand, with its bitten nails, being pressed firmly onto a round red agar culture plate by a bespectacled and white-coated researcher. A white imprint of her finger remains in the soft shiny material, a ghostly impression of her touch. The salt in the sweat on her finger has reacted with the silver in the agar plate to leave a visible white fingerprint, the mark of the disease. A different finger, this time of a manicured woman, is pressed onto the plate next, and nothing remains, as those without CF leave no mark. This test, the silver agar plate test, gained some currency early on as a screening test for the disease; any child with a visible fingerprint on the agar was suspected of having the disease if the other symptoms were present. But the fingerprint test did not quantify the amount of salt in the sweat, and di Sant' Agnese's studies suggested that the normal population might also contain some people with relatively higher amounts of salt in the sweat—higher than the average but not high enough to justify a diagnosis of cystic fibrosis.

In the same 1956 film, another child with curly brown hair, an unnamed toddler girl younger than Martha, undergoes the state-of-the-art sweat test for the time: the "bag test." The toddler sits naked on the same examination table. A six-inch-square bandage has been placed on her back, and we are shown the white gauze underneath clear plastic wrap sealed with thick white tape. She faces away from the camera as a white-sleeved hand seals the edges of the bandage. The camera cuts for a moment, and then suddenly, from stage right, a white-coated researcher enters with a large, clear plastic bag and places it over the child's head. It is with relief that we see the toddler's head pop through the plastic while the rest of the bag encases her, and the researcher lies her down on the table and ties the plastic bag in a knot below her feet. He then spreads a blue-green blanket over the girl's body, followed by a darker wool coverlet—the idea is to make her warm, so she will sweat.

After another cut, the researcher returns from stage right, removes the blankets, and pulls the plastic from the child's body. He glances somewhat sheepishly at the camera for a moment, and I realize that this is Dr. Mahmoodian! In the film he is a much younger man but still with the same kind efficiency that characterizes his work in the lab today. A voiceover—unaccented and clearly not Dr. Mahmoodian—describes the test as "very accurate and not uncomfortable for the patient." Indeed, the child does not seem bothered by the procedure, and the bandage seems to slide right off her back, indicating how much she has sweated under the blanket. The gauze under the plastic is now taken away so that the collected sweat on the gauze can be tested for sodium and chloride.

The bag test was regarded as the standard way to collect sufficient sweat in the younger child for a few years, but the film overemphasizes the simplicity of the test. A 1958 paper from Johns Hopkins describes the bag test as uncomfortable, time-consuming, and even hazardous due to the risk of inducing the same heat prostration that overcame the children admitted in the summer of 1948. The authors dismiss the bag test because of the constant monitoring required to prevent the less cooperative child, in the staid language of the medical literature, from "enacting a forceful exit from the bag." The question was how to generate and collect enough sweat in children in a reliable and simpler way. The problem was solved by two Baltimore physiologists, Gibson and Cooke, using "pilocarpine iontophoresis." Pilocarpine, a substance extracted from the stalks of a shrub in

Brazil, was known to cause increased sweating when taken orally, but it also caused drooling, cough, changes in heart rate, nausea, vomiting, and urinary retention—hardly ideal for a diagnostic test in children. Gibson and Cooke developed a method of inducing an electrical charge in the skin so that a small amount of pilocarpine would be absorbed only locally and produce sweating only in the area, thus avoiding the effects of an oral dose. This became the modern sweat test, a version of which is still the one used today.

It is this newer sweat test that Dr. Mahmoodian has just performed on Baby and for which the parents and grandparents wait in the hallway outside my office. If the test is normal, Dr. Mahmoodian will tell them directly and write up a report to send to the baby's pediatrician. The screening done on the newborn blood at the maternity hospital gives false positives, sometimes up to ten false positives for every true positive, so at that time the sweat test was the gold standard for diagnosis. In some cases, the diagnosis is made by the sweat test combined with genetic testing, and for every confirmed case genetic testing will be done, but for many families with a positive screen, the sweat test is normal, and no further testing is needed.

If the test is not normal, Dr. Mahmoodian will page me. And that is what he does today.

I received the call at my desk down the hall from Dr. Mahmoodian's office. I don't recall what I was doing, maybe reading pulmonary function tests on the hospital's awkward computer system, or perhaps trying to catch up on some dictation of clinical charts. A call from Dr. Mahmoodian is not a surprise, but it is not a daily occurrence. The number of sweat tests we do has increased in the new era of newborn screening at the maternity hospital, and most of them are normal. But today Baby's test is very abnormal—the sweat chloride values are far above the cutoff for CF, a classically positive test.

Dr. Mahmoodian does not tell the parents the test is positive. That is the job of the doctor who will follow the family forward as they join the hundreds of other families in our CF clinic. Today it is my job to welcome them to their new lives by giving them the bad news.

Life with CF is different for every family, but there are currents of sameness that run throughout their lives. For almost everyone, the memory of the day of diagnosis lingers. They will remember only part of what I say—this is true for every talk between a doctor and a patient—and the part they remember may not be right or the most important part of our conversation. If things go well today . . . but how can I use the phrase "go well" when giving this diagnosis? Better to say that if things don't go terribly, the family can start off in a good relationship with the doctors and nurses and therapists at the clinic.

The portentous nature of giving a new diagnosis of CF used to terrify me. I agonized over what I said. I ruminated over how to do it better, and I sought advice from the senior physicians.

One told me to give all the information: the physiology of the disease, the treatments, the statistics, the complications. He gave me handout to give them, with charts and photos of chest X-rays and descriptions of the all the current research protocols at the clinic.

Another told me to give the diagnosis and answer any questions, but say very little, since "they won't remember anything you say, anyway. We'll just have to end up going over it and over it again. Don't waste your time; just make them a follow-up appointment and get on with your day."

The division chief told me to tell them we would have a gene therapy to cure the disease in five years. Twenty-five years later, gene therapy has not arrived.

When I first began my fellowship in pediatric pulmonology, I thought breaking the bad news of a positive sweat test would be one of the hardest things I would ever do. Over the years I have had to deliver much worse news so many times that I no longer dread the conversation. In the beginning, I had to work to control my own sorrow over the diagnosis. But as I worked more and more with children and then young adults with CF, I have come to realize that there are far worse things that can happen to an infant, and far worse news than the diagnosis I have had to give to people with cystic fibrosis—the new acquisition of a resistant bacterium, for example, or the news that they are not a candidate for transplant, or the news that there is nothing more we can do to treat far-advanced lung disease. So my approach to giving the diagnosis has evolved to be different with every family. I talk a bit and watch their reaction, and I see what they want to know. I have given up trying to make one size fit all.

For this family, this may be the worse news they have ever gotten from a doctor. That I can handle this conversation is no consolation to them; that this is not the worst thing that can happen cannot compensate for the threat to their dream of a healthy child. I will try to make a few clear points and follow the lead of the parents, but this will turn out to be a family who wants to talk, and I would be putting out fires of fear until the very end. Everyone spoke at once except the grandfather, who was silent during the entire visit.

Hello, I'm Dr. Robinson. This is little Joseph?

"Yes, yes, I'm his mother and this is his father, and these are my parents and his father."

"Hello, Dr. Robinson."

"Hello, hello."

Hello, hello. I am one of the lung specialists. Let's go into this room where we can talk, all right? Everybody can come, yes, there are enough chairs.

Let me just say right off that the sweat test for CF is positive, confirming that Joey has cystic fibrosis.

"I knew it. I knew it! I just knew it. Didn't I say?"

"But how could it be, how could it be? He looks fine, he is fine. How can this be?"

"I knew it when the doctor told us, when we got that letter. I just knew it somehow. Oh, sweet Joey. Oh, Joey, oh."

It's going to be all right. It's going to be all right. I am here, we are all here, there are lots of people here to help you. I can answer your questions about this.

"He's going to die? He'll never get married and never have kids and he's going to be the in the hospital all the time and he's . . ."

No, no, now wait a minute. Let's talk. Let's talk. He's going to be okay. I have lots of patients with CF who do just fine. Some of them are older than I am.

"Oh God, oh God, where did he get this? Did he get this from me? Did I do something, someone in my family, someone gave this to him . . . the obstetrician did tests! And the ultrasounds and all of that and he was fine when he was born, and she said we were fine. She said everything was A-OK. She said we were fine!"

"Well, it's not from our family."

"What do you mean—it's not in our family either!"

It's from both families—Joey got one copy of the gene from both parents. That's how this works.

"What if we have more children?"

"Can he go to school?"

"Are you sure about the test? Can't you do it again? Can't the test be wrong? He looks fine, eating and sleeping and everything, just fine."

"What about his cousins? What about his aunts and uncles? Will all the babies in the family have this thing?"

"What can he eat? The internet said he needed special food! What kind of food? How can I give him medicine, he's so little? How can we do all this?"

We have a whole clinic here to help you, doctors, nurses, social workers, physical therapists, nutritionists, all people who will help you. We can answer every question. We will help you with all of this.

"But are you sure? What is the test is wrong? What if this is all a mistake?"

"I knew there was something wrong from the moment I read the pediatrician's letter. I knew, but I didn't want to say anything."

"Does he need to go in the hospital today? Can we take him home?"

"Will he be in the hospital long? Doesn't he need medicine right now, to go ahead and start?"

"Oh, I can't take this. I can't take it. Poor little Joey."

It's all going to be all right. I am going to help you. We are all going to help you. He doesn't need to be in the hospital right now. We will set it up so you come to the clinic tomorrow morning and we will get started on everything. There is a lot to learn, but we will help you.

"What about his brain? Will he be able to walk?"

Yes, yes, his brain works fine—no problems with the brain in CF. He can go to school and run and play and do lots of things. In fact, we will encourage him to run and exercise.

After about twenty minutes the family had exhausted their first round of questions, the ones that seemed to run out of them under pressure, and they all sat silently, one grandmother looking at me expectantly and the other looking at the baby. The grandfather sat quietly, waiting, perhaps, to be called upon to do something useful; he seemed to me then like the sort of man who wants a job to do. The parents and the grandmothers had hardly listened to each other and I doubted they had heard much of the specifics. I hadn't provided much information, hadn't gone into the meds or the different symptoms or the prognosis or anything much. But they seemed to know enough for the moment.

Now, in the middle of the silence after the avalanche of talking, the father began to cry. Great tears ran down his face without sound as he hugged his wife and looked down at the sleeping infant in her arms. He bent further and further over her lap as if to envelop the baby, to cover his son with his protection. I leaned forward across the table.

I know this is hard. I know it is. But you are going to be okay. There are lots of people here who can help you, and we have seen every possible problem that can come up and we know how to help. There are lots of other families who have been through what you are going through right now, and I can arrange for you to talk to them if you want, any time. There will always be someone here to help you, any time.

The father began to sob loudly, and his mother reached over to give him a tissue, and we sat silently for what seemed like five minutes but was less than one. He wiped his face and took another tissue and blew his nose, and then cried some more. The second time he blew his nose he began to calm down and smile at his son. He blew his nose loudly one final time and then laughed as though startled.

"What the hell? I think I blew my nose out through my eye? What was that?" And he laughed again.

His wife said, "What are you talking about?" with a smile breaking onto her face. And he said, "When I blew my nose I felt a puff of air on my eye! I did!"

And then he laughed again and everyone else began to smile, acknowledging that it was okay to cry now, and okay to laugh, and we could go back to being ourselves. I told him yes, there is a connection between the nose and the tear ducts, and that happens to people when they cry, and they were all laughing by now and the baby had woken up and was looking at his mother and father. I knew they were going to be all right.

It took ten years for the events of the hot summer of 1948 to be translated into an efficient and effective diagnostic test for Dorothy

Andersen's disease. Andersen, who died in 1963, remained somewhat suspicious of the sweat findings, tending to emphasize other aspects of the disease in the diagnostic process. But the insight of increased salt in the sweat of children with CF would change more than just the diagnosis of the disease. The sweat abnormalities would prove to be the key to studying the microscopic changes and mutations responsible for the current understanding of the disease.

There is at least one more pertinent question to be asked about the story of sweat and cystic fibrosis. Why did it take the extremes of dehydration for Andersen and her colleagues to be curious about sweating in patients with CF? Most children with CF sweat far more than other children, and this abnormal sweating is noticed by almost every parent of a child with the disease today. It surely would have been noted by the parents of some of the sixty children seen in the Babies Hospital clinic by Andersen in the decade between 1938 and 1948. Paul Quinton, a prominent CF researcher born in 1944 who has CF, reports that his family used to joke about how his T-shirts in the summer were so wet and salty that they rusted the metal hangers—and this was a family joke before Quinton was ever diagnosed with the disease. Mothers routinely report now that their infants taste salty when kissed, and children with CF can form shiny deposits on their shirt collars and socks in the summer months. It is not something a mother wouldn't notice. So did they report it? There is no mention of sweating in any of the many clinical reports that followed Andersen's 1938 paper, and no mention of abnormal sweating as a clinical symptom at all until the mid-1950s, after di Sant' Agnese published his work.

The best answer is that the mothers in the clinic answered the questions they were asked. Other aspects of the physical and clinical histories of the children with cystic fibrosis were obsessively described in Andersen's work, so the absence of this one very odd detail seems remarkable until we remember that doctors, like all of us, see what we expect to see. The unexpected is often invisible. Doctors do not draw the picture of a new illness on a blank canvas. Anderson, the pathologist, failed to recognize a trait that could not be detected on autopsy, and di Sant' Agnese doubted what he had seen because experts told him it was "impossible." But the children still sweated, and mothers still tasted salt in their kisses, even if no doctor noticed.

WHITE COAT, BLACK HABIT

1. I Am Defeated by the Smell of Blood

In the last hour of the day in a coal mine ten miles out of town, a top-mounted conveyor caught a man between the belt and the roof of the mineshaft, scraping his body along the jagged seam. Only his helmet kept the machine from crushing his skull. Someone shut off the diesel engine and pulled him from the grip of the mechanism, and someone else got him to the surface, his moans echoing though the small shaft, so oddly quiet now the drills had stopped.

The EMTs rolled him into the ER on a narrow stretcher and placed him on the trauma bed set like an altar in the middle of the treatment room. The nurse put EKG leads on his chest and an IV catheter in his left arm, checked his pulse and his pupils. Only once she was sure he was stable did she begin to peel off the bandages wrapped around his chest. A wave of blood crested onto his plaid shirt; she clamped a thick white bandage over the wound and called for the doctor, "Hey, back here, *now*."

I stood useless outside the door of the treatment room. I was a volunteer in the ER, twenty-three years old, the year before I started medical school. The smell of so much blood, the shirt stained three shades of red, and the low moans of the miner collided against me. My head seemed to lift off my neck and float in the aroma of blood while the hallway jerked sideways and spun forward. My back felt like it was rising toward the ceiling while my forehead crouched on the green linoleum floor. The ceiling lights narrowed into a spiky cone surrounded by ink, binoculars turned backward. I could feel my feet inside my socks.

I sat down heavily on a low metal stool, my head in my hands.

I thought: *Do not fall over. Do not pass out.*

I thought: *Do not make a fool of yourself.*

I thought: *You will never survive as a doctor.*

2. I See the Molecules of God

When I was seven I could see the molecules of God. Round circles of shining gold filled the bars of the cross behind the altar at our church, forty-eight perfect circles aligned in hollow rows, and I thought they were the building blocks of holiness. God was made of golden molecules, divinely symmetric and glowing above my head. The shining metal was lit with indirect light; I could not get the cross or the circles in focus all at once, like a streetlight on a rainy night. It made sense: my human eyes were too week to see perfection. The cross floated in front of the wall behind the altar, held up by means invisible to me. The molecules of God's holiness held the cross in place, and I had no choice but to look up at this solid, inexplicable presence, the buoyant proof of living divinity.

I didn't take Jesus very seriously. He was a pale man in a pastel bathrobe on a filmstrip and we only saw him in Sunday School. Jesus smelled too much like paste to be a serious part of the divine world. He was full of advice, but the men in my childhood were full of advice, none of which I could follow: *keep your eyes on the ball, keep your eyes on the target, don't think so hard, don't be so sensitive.* Golden molecules of God made more sense than any of that. Jesus said *Drink ye all of this*, and I thought he meant you had to drink the whole cup of wine at once, which no one seemed to do, and anyway this command sounded like Jesus telling us to clean our plates.

What I loved when I was a boy was the language of the service, the *thee* and *thou* and the rhythm of the words, but especially the sameness of the words every week. Morning Prayer was the first play I ever learned by heart. As I got older, like everyone who has seen a play over and over, I became a connoisseur and critic of the performance. I could tell when the minister said the words with hesitation or added some new inflection. I cringed when he didn't have the right solemnity in his voice. I thought of the service as poetry. The only poet I knew was A. A. Milne, and I was a great reader aloud of his poetry. I won a prize for poetry recitation every year from first grade until fifth, except in sixth grade when I wanted to recite a poem by Robert Service about how Adam did not have a belly button but was not allowed to because it might confuse the children in the lower grades. If I hadn't read the poems just so, I wouldn't have won the prizes, would I?

These words were written down centuries before I was born, and if the words were said out of turn or in the wrong tone of voice, then the holiness might not descend. If we didn't get it just right, the golden circles might just be metal, and the church might be just a big room, and Sunday morning might be nothing special.

I practiced not needing the prayer book, because I thought God would want me to know his words by heart. I criticized those adults who still used the book, including my father and mother, and hoped God would have patience with them for not studying enough. I wanted to have the words of the prayers flow out of me, come forth as if commanded, so that I could feel their meaning, even if I did not understand them all. The words were a script for talking to God, and I wanted to get my lines right.

3. I Cut Open My First Patient

In the dissection room at the age of twenty-four, a week into my first year of medical school, I surprised myself by being unmoved by the proximity of twelve dead humans. I was wrong that evening in the ER: I was never truly squeamish again. Dissection didn't bother me at all. Gloved-up and holding a new scalpel in my right hand, I made a line straight down the sternum and then laterally across the top of the chest near the collarbones—I had not yet learned to call them *clavicles*. I peeled back the cool gray skin to reveal the thin flap of muscle called the *platysma*, a word that even now sounds perfect in my mouth, the second syllable emphasized in the same manner as *epiphany*.

True, the smell was bad, and it seemed to cling to me. The aroma of formaldehyde lived inside my nostrils, and sometimes I thought I smelled preservative every time I blinked. But the senses exhaust themselves, and a few breaths on entering the room each day were all it took to no longer to notice the reek while I worked on the body.

Our cadaver was a large bald man with a body shaped like mine is today: flabby and round. He was hairless except for his groin. I am anything but hairless, so I will be a polar bear to his walrus, if they still do human dissections by the time I am a candidate. There will be one other difference: our cadaver's eyes were empty sockets, cotton balls with white flame-like wisps licking the air through his eyelids, his corneas harvested to give sight to someone still living. My incipient cataracts will insure that medical students will be able to look right into the windows of my soul, should they feel the need.

To cut open a stranger's dead body you have to turn off your imagination. You have to refuse to ponder the indignity of death. You have to focus on the usefulness of the human husk. What once was a person is now a lesson plan. These were people, but now you display them for a grade good enough to pass and, you hope, for some benefit to humans you have not met. Your cadaver is your first patient, and you are not yet a doctor. I spent a lot of time picking globs of fat away from something I thought was the vagus nerve, only to discover that I had been carefully uncovering a strand of connective tissue so irrelevant as to be nameless in the textbooks.

Near the end of the months of dissection, the body looks very much worse for wear, usually cut in half through the spinal cord so that the different student teams can work on the upper and lower body at once. You discard all the organs and tissues already examined so that the body shrinks each week, and what is left falls apart in your hands, shredded as it is by all the poking and prying of your tools.

I was solid now, fearful of failing but not of fainting. I had come to understand how to distance myself from my imagination. I began to reconfigure frailty into curable sickness. I was becoming practical. I was learning to see people as bodies.

4. I Put on the White Coat

Before the third year of medical school, students buy their first white coat. We had to be sure to buy the right sort of coat because the hierarchy of the hospital was based on the length of the white coat. Woe be unto anyone who wore a coat of the wrong length. Students and residents wore the shortest ones, the length of a sports coat, but often short-sleeved because of the heat; the fellows, one step closer to divinity, wore coats that descended to just above the knee. The attending physicians, the walking gods, had coats that fell below the knee and were spotless, made of a thicker cotton and washed-starched-pressed to a stiff sheen for them by the hospital laundry. Their names were embroidered in red cursive above the left breast pocket as proof of their magisterial rank.

Medical students' coats were made of thin cotton bleached hard white and had large flapless pockets on both sides, as well as a large breast pocket for pens and the ubiquitous eye chart with a ruler on the side that every student carried but never used, except when the attending wanted to prove to you that your measurement of a wound edge was imprecise. We always needed a pen or two, because as medical students we weren't really allowed to do much other than write things down, and no one lends a medical student a pen in the hospital.

In their coat pockets, the residents carried paper sheets folded lengthwise and sticking up under the arm of the coat; these were their sign-out sheets for all the patients on the ward. The residents would recite from them during the liturgy of morning report with the sing-song efficiency used by doctors to talk to one another about the bodies under their care. A fellow's coat held similar lists, but the fellows were expected to memorize their patient lists and used the sheets on rounds only to check an obscure lab value. If the information was important, they should know it by heart. Nothing graced the pockets of an attending's coat, not paper, not a pen; their coat pockets were often still starched closed. If they needed something, it would be handed to them.

On the left sleeve of our white coats, just below the shoulder seam, we were instructed to sew a blue square with the name of the medical school on it in small letters. The school made it clear that it was a matter of ethics: we must have that patch to identify us to everyone as not yet a real doctor. Of course, no patient could see that patch, nor would anyone who was sick take the time or effort to read the finely sewn script lettering. We were doctors as far as the patients knew, but peons to anyone who mattered.

5. I Consider the Black Habit

I became a doctor, and twenty years later at age forty-three, I wanted to become a monk as well. I wanted to put on the black habit and white rope belt of The Society of St. John the Evangelist, an Episcopalian order. About fifteen monks lived in the monastery. For one year, every day before going to work at the hospital, I went to the Morning Prayer service at the monastery. Outsiders like me, men and women, could come to the monks' services and sit to the side of the central aisle. That year, I was the only one who came regularly, or so I remember; bound up as I was in mind and heart, I would not have noticed anyone else. We spoke and sang the service together, though I mumbled in exhaustion some mornings.

I wanted to join the monks because in their presence I thought I could speak to something like God. I wanted to leave the relentlessly contemporary language of medicine for half an hour and rest inside the solemn vocabulary of my childhood. It was a relief to return to the Book of Common Prayer.

The yearly cycle of the Psalms, at least for me, turned upon a wheel forged by certainty about human nature. During one week, the monks and I might beg a vengeful God to smite our heathen enemies in ways almost too terrible to say aloud: leave them yowling in pits of oily despair, rend their limbs, break their ungodly teeth, cover them with running sores and pinching pains. Through the Psalms, I might delight in the suffering of the ungodly and join my voice to others to God in the expectation that He might hound them trembling from their strongholds and cast them like dirt into the streets.

In the following week the monks and I might leave off calling down plagues and instead chant our frustration at our human smallness, at the drudgery of being in a life "waxen old with heaviness." The next month we would sing about how hard it is, and how glorious, to see the mystery of the heavens from our pitiful vantage in this ordinary world. Later we would wonder at the heavy burden of faith, how poorly we are equipped to shoulder it, and how often we stumble under the weight. A few months later we would speak all week only of waiting in fervent patience for the solace of a God who might provide something so rare and wonderful that it required its own compound word: *loving-kindness*.

I heard these verses with new ears, spoke them with a voice grown tired, and wrapped up my soul in the new opportunity to understand myself. I thought I had found the words to show me the golden molecules again. I returned to the monastery each morning like an addict.

When I was twenty I volunteered to work over the summer break from college in a Cambodian refugee camp in 1980, and I returned home so changed by the experience that I decided to become a doctor. My father had also been away from home at age twenty in the summer of 1943, in the US Army in the Gulf of Gela in Sicily. I knew nothing of his experience in war, how it might have changed him; I only learned these details sixty years later from his obituary. Until he died, I had never seen the picture of him in uniform, a dark wool uniform jacket and tightly knotted khaki tie, clean-shaven, an officer's hat tilted to the right on top of a close haircut, a hint of a smile at the left corner of his mouth. I have now looked at that photograph a dozen times, but I cannot discern the emotion in the soldier's eyes.

My father and I never talked about his summer of 1943. We never talked about his fear or his courage, or about the lives we hold inside ourselves. By the time of college I was a near stranger to my parents, though neither side acknowledged that fact.

While working in the camp, I wrote my parents every week on pale-blue Aerogram paper. Many years later, after my parents died, I searched for those letters among all the boxes of things my mother saved: Christmas cards, old catalogues, menus of the parties she hosted, condolence letters from decades-old deaths, photos and descriptions of every trip taken, and plans for all the trips not taken. I still haven't found the letters.

I do have the one letter my family mailed to me in the camp. It was thicker than expected, full of ordinary paper and not the tissue-like Aerogram, and the address was not in my mother's rounded and looping script but in my father's precise slant.

I opened the letter in the heat of the small room where I slept under a mosquito net. The letter was a folded copy of my college transcript, three As and two A minuses, with a note in my father's crisp cursive next to the lower grades: "What happened? Love, Dad."

In the years that followed, the story of The Only Letter from Home was a favorite at dinner parties. *What sort of man was your father?* people would ask. *What was he thinking with that letter?* The trite interpretation is that he cared only for my grades, but surely there was some attempt at connection lurking in effort of sending a letter at all. Was it like the clippings and wedding invitations my mother sent me over the years, always about some schoolmate, someone my mother wrongly thought might be my friend? The message in those letters was as subtle as a slap: you ought to have more friends, why aren't you married, when are you going to move back home? But as for the one letter my father sent, I cannot say now what it really meant. Was it his warning never to rest in the struggle of life? Was it his warning against pride? Was it notice that I, like everyone else, would always be found wanting, like the note on the wall to Nebuchadnezzar I had heard my father describe so many times?

Or was it a joke, as my mother later insisted, a joke I failed to see because, as she put it, I was "too sensitive." I could imagine situations in which this letter might be funny—a *what have you done for me lately* sort of joke. But my father had not earned the right to tell that joke. That joke had to stand on a foundation of care—*you know I love you, you know I am proud of you, and this is funny because you know that.* No such foundation existed.

7. I Think I Am a Perfect Candidate

The Psalms we chanted at the monastery knew the seduction of vengeance. They knew that all of us have at some point wished a boss, a bomber, a professor, a colleague, or a parent to be cast down by a ferocious God into a fiery pit of damnation so that we the righteous may finally triumph. The Psalms know that sometimes we are children who send prayers like wishes up to a Santa Claus figure in the sky, and that at other times we humans talk to God with "the honesty of a drunk," as Anne Sexton wrote, giving the Almighty the what for and telling him how to run the universe.

That year at Morning Prayer, I needed to say my human desires out loud instead of putting them privately into the lap of a therapist. I wanted to announce my nature under the cover of anonymity in a vaulted stone room with strangers in black robes. All of us rage against our enemies, and want vengeance, and it seemed to me better to admit this in unison using the beautiful and strange words of a few centuries ago than to imagine that my sufferings were unique or that I was the first one to rail against fate. Reading the words of the Psalms in a small dark church with fifteen other men reminded me how foolish it was to think that the solutions to human suffering are a simply a matter of better laws and more justice, better diagnoses and stronger treatments. Our suffering is part of us. My suffering is part of me. The Psalms join me to my species, bringing me into the fold of humanity, if not the fold of believers. I could hear the past and the present in the voices of these men in robes and rope belts. I could join them entreating the most powerful thing into the universe to come down here, reward me for my faithfulness and honor, revenge my wrongs, give me solace. It didn't seem delusional to wish that my smallness and fragility had a purpose beyond the turning of the days. I knew there was no being in the sky, no power above me, nothing supernatural that has a consciousness to which I might matter, nothing that could come to my punishment or rescue. But I wished there were.

I was tired when I was forty-three, and I felt lost in the middle of my work and my life. The marks of success I had gained had meaning only for themselves: research grants that would lead to publications that would lead to more grants that would lead to promotions I didn't care about. I was tired of working so hard to make all this matter to me with the same fervor that it mattered to everyone else.

The reasons I became a doctor seemed to me then to be a mix of selfishness and suspect altruism. I had wanted to make the world a better place, but I had also wanted an escape from myself. I had wanted to join a group dedicated to serving an unbidden self-sacrifice, but I also wanted to put on a cloak of respectability every morning in order to justify my own smallness, my fears and inadequacies. Medicine could be a sword for the sick and a shield for myself. But by that time I had realized the dullness of my sword against the suffering of others. The shield of the white coat could not protect me.

Becoming a monk seemed to offer what I wanted then, a life free of the noise of the world so that I could hear myself in the echo of days. So in the dim light of winter mornings I called upon a being I didn't believe in to destroy those who weren't really my enemies, knowing I was only calling on myself to let the disheartened residue of living flow out of my mouth and into the air. The monks offered more than just religion. Their lives seemed to embrace the combination of solitude and union I craved. At Morning Prayer they did not pause to shake hands with the other people in the pews, as so many services do; they did not break the chain of the liturgy with the "passing of the peace." I imagined that like me they didn't think of peace as something passed from person to person by a scheduled gesture. Peace worth having is elusive; it hides from workaday politeness. I thought I felt it in the rests and repeats of those morning services.

I depended on the power of the monks' voices to free me from the burden of being alone in the world, and most days it worked. After a few minutes I could let go of the fact that I didn't have any real enemies and didn't believe in some Being in the Sky and remember what it felt like to be small and frail and at the whim of a life I hardly understood. I imagined those men of the past speaking the words just as I was, using the power of collective language to remind ourselves that though we have not come completely out of the darkness of our hearts, solace can still arise from shared invocation. Saying it together meant we were not alone. I had no real idea what the monks thought or felt, no idea whether they said the words in the grip of nothing greater than wilted habit or if, like me, the words were searing themselves into their hearts as soon as they left their mouths. I never asked, because I did not want to hear the answer. I thought I had enough answer for myself.

When I was forty-three, I was a perfect monastic candidate: single, no attachments, debt-free, and in need of humility. The three monastic vows didn't really worry me. I thought I would have no problem with chastity, because sex and desire had not turned out well and it would be a relief to get rid of them. I could get used to their comfortable version of poverty, since the monastery was beautiful and on a river in my cultured city. I wasn't so sure about obedience. *Obedience*, as one of the monks put it to me, *is a bitch*.

I wrote a letter to the brother in charge of the novices, Brother Jonathan, about my thoughts of becoming a monk.

I have thought deeply about why I am drawn to caring for children and families for whom there is no cure. I used to say to myself (and to others when asked) that I could do this work because I believed in Heaven, but this just does not explain it, and anyway I am not so sure of Heaven. What seems special or important is my sometime ability simply to watch and wait, a "sometime ability" because it is not easy or always possible for me. I am beginning to understand how important it is when I can do it—how hard it is to wait with someone, and not to try to rescue them or distract yourself with some other task. I am not the first to recognize both the importance and the difficulty of waiting. Even the apostles in Gethsemane cannot wait with Jesus when He asks them to; they want to fight, to raise swords against the approach of death, but when it is not their action but their presence which is requested, they fall asleep and leave the suffering Jesus to sit alone. Later, only John and Mary can wait at the foot of the cross—how hard this must have been, how easy it would have been to give in to their despair and make their waiting into a story about themselves instead of about the one who is suffering. This sometime ability to wait with my patients and their families is a gift from a giver who I need to search for, someone I need to know, though I am wary of the pride which lurks behind the sense of being given a gift, wary of thinking that I am special.

I am trying to understand how God figures in my work. I suppose I started noticing the change at the funerals—when I sat there, in church for the first time in years, I began to remember what being in church felt like, and to remember with my heart being in the presence of something or someone greater and larger. I think this something greater is God. I have started going to church again, but it is hard, and I admit it unnerves me. Now often in church I am so moved, so full of something I cannot put words to, that I find myself with tears on my face, my heart so full it feels like it will leave my chest. It is a hard and powerful feeling, not a "feel good" feeling. It is not joy, nor is it happiness, but a sense of the nearness of something strong, a connection which I cannot describe clearly.

So why think of being a monk? I am no Merton. I am touched (but I want to write "refreshed" instead) by your Rule: "We will recognize that the concern with individualistic fulfillment and private security that prevails in our culture is a trap from which we are being set free." And "We also need to let go of any grasping for immediate results; much of what the grace of God achieves through us will be entirely hidden from our eyes."

I can see now that the release from expectation was part of the lure of the monastery. The monks knew we cannot add to the good of the world without work and struggle, but they had decided to struggle together in a way foreign to the world of the doctor. They wanted to share the work and never take credit individually for the things that happened by the grace of something more powerful than any one of them. The monks knew that fate or something like it ruled the course of lives far more than the temporary repair of broken bodies.

8. I Sit in Silence and Make a Decision

I spent a week at the monastery in silence with a group of other men who were also thinking about becoming monks, going to service five times a day and eating together in the big refectory, listening to one of the monks read a book on Scottish history at lunch and dinner. I was surprised that being silent was not a chore for me, and there were no moments when I felt the need to speak; my life was so full of talking, so full of arguing about the right thing to do, so full of the noise of everyone getting his words in and no one listening. That week there were no comical miming moments when I could not get the salt when I needed it. The monks' rule was clear that speaking when necessary was permitted during the periods of chosen silence. They wanted you to think about necessity differently. Outside of the monastery, I lived in a world where speaking was hard to distinguish from arguing: my diagnosis is correct, this treatment is needed, this grant deserves money, I am worth a promotion. All speech had an agenda of persuasion. Inside the monastery, I thought, there would be nothing to argue for or against, nothing to gain by insistence or assertion, no truth to prove.

I spent most of that week in silence on a hard chair in the cool stone sanctuary, a scarecrow trying to run through all the words in my head, to imagine myself as innocent enough to abide, or quiet enough to keep watch. But my mind was full of talking, an inexhaustible supply of language. I got only partial relief during the services. The words gave me distraction but not replacement; I could not experience the words of the service as a single scroll of meaning in my head, because every sentence asked me to think about it, asked me whether I really believed the words I was saying. I could not live inside the language of the Book as I had done as a child.

But how I wanted to! I wanted to feel God as close as the ceiling. I was tired of trying to talk the world into solid being with ordinary words and useless precision. I wanted to let the words of my childhood convince my adult self that the molecules of God were real enough. I wanted to give up the parts of myself that I didn't like and adopt someone else's way of living. I wanted to recite the poetry of the service and be done with talking. I wanted to trust in something other than myself.

At night I sat at the desk in my cell on the third floor listening to George Harrison on my iPod. Not very monastic. The plaintive certainty of *All Things Must Pass* seemed an instruction manual and a consolation. Harrison was warning me not to listen too closely to the material world, that darkness and sorrow was pervasive but not permanent, that connection without manipulation was still possible. I wanted to have his sort of confidence. But I didn't.

What am I doing here, I thought, *spending my rare vacation in a room with a single bed with scratchy sheets and a bendy table lamp, taking tepid showers down the hall at 5:00 a.m.? What am I doing in this anachronism, a nineteenth-century place in a twenty-first-century world, repeating the words of people who lived in a time before antibiotics when all my patients would have died in infancy? Who am I to think that my own salvation is worth ignoring the lives of others?* And yet each morning I was moved to near tears by the service, by the human longing and simplicity of the words, the shared voices. *There is something here*, I thought, *something I need so deeply, and it surrounds me like incense, pungent and powerful enough to quiet my mind.*